For my colleague and friend,
Robert Trisco
with the esteem and affection

John Tracy Ellis

March 29, 1989

FAITH AND LEARNING

MELVILLE STUDIES IN CHURCH HISTORY

FROM

The Department of Church History
The Catholic University of America

EDITED BY

Nelson H. Minnich

EDITORIAL COMMITTEE

MELVILLE STUDIES IN CHURCH HISTORY
VOLUME I

FAITH AND LEARNING

A CHURCH HISTORIAN'S STORY

John Tracy Ellis

UNIVERSITY
PRESS OF
AMERICA

Lanham • New York • London

The Department of
Church History

The Catholic University
of America

Copyright © **1989** by

University Press of America,® Inc.

4720 Boston Way
Lanham, MD 20706

3 Henrietta Street
London WC2E 8LU England

Printed in the United States of America

British Cataloging in Publication Information Available

Co-published by arrangement with The Department of Church History,
The Catholic University of America

Library of Congress Cataloging-in-Publication Data

Ellis, John Tracy, 1905–
Faith and learning : a church historian's story / John Tracy Ellis.
p. cm.—(Melville studies in church history ; v. 1)
Includes bibliographical references and index.
1. Ellis, John Tracy, 1905–   . 2. Church historians—United
States—Biography. 3. Catholic Church—United States—Clergy—
Biography. I. Catholic University of America. Dept. of Church
History. II. Title. III. Series.
BR139.E55A3   1988
270'.092'4—dc 19
[B]   88–27678 CIP
ISBN 0–8191–7214–6 (alk. paper)

IN LOVING MEMORY
OF
MY COLLEGE TEACHER, FELLOW HISTORIAN,
AND DEAR FRIEND
EDWARD V. CARDINAL, C.S.V.
1897-1981

Acknowledgment

Monsignor John Tracy Ellis' autobiography is the first in a projected series of studies in church history. This series bears the name of Dr. Annabelle M. Melville, an alumna of the Catholic University of America, distinguished historian of the Catholic Church in America, and Commonwealth Professor Emerita of History, Bridgewater State College, Massachusetts, since 1977. Her generous benefactions to the Department of Church History make possible the publication of a series of monographs featuring the work of the faculty, students, and alumni/ae of this department. It is hoped that these studies will carry on the tradition of exacting scholarship and deep love for the history of the Church so well exemplified in the career and writings of Dr. Melville.

Table of Contents

A Prefatory Note

This memoir is in no need of an extended preface; its character is too obvious to require detailed explanation. Yet a word of introduction may prove useful by way of telling something of its origin and its purpose. The idea for such a work arose with Professor Nelson H. Minnich, Chairman of the Department of Church History, who thought it might help younger men and women setting out on a program of training to become church historians. How much it may have fulfilled that purpose only they and others can tell. I am deeply indebted to Dr. Minnich for having worked out the details concerning the publication of this monograph, and for suggestions concerning its title as well. Over the years I have found it profitable to read the reminiscences of ecclesiastical historians such as David Knowles and Owen Chadwick of England, and of John Gilmary Shea and Peter Guilday, the founding fathers, so to speak, of my own discipline, American Catholic history. Perhaps this memoir may serve a similar end.

In writing this brief work I have had occasion to reflect on how much I owe to so many who taught, counseled, and inspired me as I traveled the long road extending over sixty years since the beginning of graduate studies in 1927 to the present. For I am still benefiting from the example and encouragement of colleagues such as that once given by the dear and lamented friend to whom this work is dedicated, as well as to a number of living fellow church historians such as my former student and friend, Joseph P. Chinnici, O.F.M., associate professor of church history in the Graduate Theological Union in Berkeley, who took time from a very busy life to read these chapters and to improve them with helpful suggestions.

My lifetime study of church history has deepened both my knowledge and my love for the Church, even if it has not in all particulars lifted the veil of mystery that surrounds her. In that regard I would echo the words of Cardinal Newman when he declared:

> A number of answers can be given to the question, What is the Church? We are far from saying that in so complicated a question *only* one, or perhaps that any *one*, is right and true; but whatever is right, whatever wrong, surely we must go to history for the information.[1]

John Tracy Ellis

The Catholic University of America
September 20, 1987

---

[1]John Henry Newman, *Essays Critical and Historical* (New York, 1897) II, 253.

CHAPTER I

How It Began

"It is the first time that I have ever attempted anything which was intended to be in part a serious autobiographical essay."[1] That sentence written in 1964 was contained in a contribution requested by the editor of *The Catholic Historical Review* for the journal's golden jubilee issue of January, 1965. I entitled the article, "Reflections of an Ex-Editor," having resigned the editorship of that quarterly after a tenure of nearly twenty-two years. I shall have occasion to refer again to this article in what follows; I mention it here simply to locate the time and place where I first published anything of an autobiographical character.

While I would wish to make it clear that I am far from being a true specialist in the thought of Cardinal Newman, such as was true of my lamented friend, Charles Stephen Dessain (1908-1976) of the Birmingham Oratory, I have more than once stated that aside from Jesus and His Mother no one has had more influence on my life and thought than Newman. I suspect his name will appear fairly frequently in this memoir, but I make no apology for that since he so often expressed ideas in precisely the way I should wish to have expressed them, and that with a literary grace that far

---

[1] John Tracy Ellis, "Reflections of an Ex-Editor," *The Catholic Historical Review* L (January, 1965), 469.

surpassed anything that I could achieve. Let the following illustrate what I mean, a statement wherein Newman touched on the factors that influence the lives of all of us in one way or another. As I read these words I thought how appropriate they were for setting the stage, so to speak, of this memoir on my role as a church historian. Newman put the point in this way:

> Let a person who trusts he is on the whole serving God acceptably, look back upon his past life, and he will find how critical were moments and acts, which at the time seemed the most indifferent: as for instance the school he was sent to as a child, the occasion of his falling in with those persons who have most benefited him, the accidents which determined his calling or his prospects, whatever they were. God's hand is ever over his own, and he leads them forward by ways they know not of.[2]

Obviously, the schools to which we were sent and the persons we fell in with have influenced each of us for weal or for woe. In a recent rereading of seven chapters of personal memoirs written nearly twenty years ago as a preparation for the present work, I sensed the temptation to go over that ground once again, a temptation that must be avoided here since the request made by Nelson H. Minnich, Chairman of our Department of Church History, was for a memoir on my role as an historian and not for a general review of my life.

Yet something must be said of those early years. In the lives of some historians the school to which they were sent became of paramount importance to their future career, for example, Saint Bede (c. 672-735) being sent as a youth to the twin abbeys of Jarrow and Wearmouth where the splendid library collections of that seventh-century monastery were a

---

[2]John Henry Newman, *Parochial and Plain Sermons* (London, 1875) IV, 261.

prime incentive for the talented author of the *Ecclesiastical History of England*. In like manner when Caesar Baronius (1538-1607), church historian and future cardinal, 'fell in' with Saint Philip Neri (1515-1595) it was the latter's influence that prompted Baronius to undertake to refute the Lutheran work, *Centuriae Magdeburgenses,* and thus led to Baronius' multi-volume *Annales Ecclesiastici*. And among the 'accidents which determined his calling' for Henry Adams (1838-1918) was being born into a highly educated and cultivated family where literature and history were held in great esteem.

To none of these circumstances could I lay claim. I was born and raised in the little town of Seneca, Illinois, located about seventy miles southwest of Chicago in the Diocese of Peoria. Neither Saint Patrick's School nor Seneca High School where my first decade (1911-1921) of formal instruction was received was noted for more than an elementary survey of American and European history, the character and content of which left no lasting impression or served to cultivate any special taste. Nor was the environment of northern Illinois of a particularly historical kind, allowing for its having been traversed by French explorers and missionaries two and a half centuries before. And the nearest alleged historic spot, Starved Rock, Illinois' first state park, about thirty-five miles to the west of Seneca, with its story of Indians having been driven up the rock, surrounded, and left to starve, turned out to be nothing more than an oft-repeated fabrication with no factual foundation.

In a word, I can now recall no person, place, or circumstance that turned me toward a love of history before my junior year in college. My father liked to read western stories and novels, but having dropped out of high school at the end of his first year, his reading tastes did not include serious history, and my mother, a high school graduate, never cultivated a love of reading. My future avocation was not, therefore, a result of family influence and home training. My last two years of secondary school were spent at Saint Viator Academy in Bourbonnais, Illinois, a small institution about fifty miles from Seneca which had been founded by the Clerics of Saint Viator in 1865. Following my graduation from the academy in 1923, I entered Saint Viator College that September and continued on there until June 14, 1927, when my fourteen classmates and I received our bachelor of arts degrees, with Eleanor Roy, the first girl to graduate from the college, taking top honors and with one other classmate and myself coming up behind with a *magna cum laude* citation.

Thinking of early factors that influenced my future role as an historian, two professors at Saint Viator College had a notable part in directing me toward that academic discipline. These two men were Fathers Thomas J. Lynch (1894-1963) and Edward V. Cardinal, C.S.V. (1897-1981). The former taught English as his principal field, but he supplemented those courses with one in modern European history. At the time he did not have any formal training in either field beyond his A.B. degree. What he lacked in graduate instruction he made up in a measure by wide reading and personal study. In his early thirties, when I came to know him, this Irish-born man was of medium height with a broad handsome face and bright blue eyes. He was the first person of my acquaintance whose range of reading was quite remarkable. He seemed to have read all the classics of English literature while at the same time absorbing a good number of biographies of leading historical figures such as Richelieu, Louis XIV, and Napoleon.

Tom Lynch, or 'The Turk,' as we called him behind his back, had the good sense to work his students very hard; in fact, in that regard he was known as the toughest professor on the college faculty. Once I had elected to major in English I had reason to know, for he read carefully and critically commented on our term papers. A grade of B from Lynch was considered something of a distinction, and an occasional A a badge of honor. Sensing that he meant business we probably worked harder for his classes than for any other professor, and it was this steady drilling in English that accounted for whatever clarity and facility I developed in writing. Whether or not I had Lynch's direction for my first printed efforts that appeared in the students' journal, *The Viatorian,* and which were entitled "The Elizabethan Age of Literature" (1923) and a salute to Chicago's first cardinal, George Mundelein, called "Our Cardinal" (1924), I cannot now remember. That was certainly true of my bachelor's thesis, "George Meredith, the Novelist of Manners." Apart entirely from his history courses, I owed a debt of gratitude to Tom Lynch for not only introducing me to the best in English literature, but as well for helping me, as I have said, to develop an acceptable writing style that has stood me in good stead throughout my life.

Let me turn now to the contribution that Tom Lynch made to awakening my love of history. The prime consideration here was the captivating manner in which he lectured. He was extraordinarily articulate and seemingly never at a loss for a word or phrase by which to describe vividly an event or to delineate a personal character. Pacing up and down the room with not so much as a note in his hand, he caught my imagination; he not only caught it, he fired it to a degree that I almost felt myself present at the event he was describing. To employ a tired expression, Lynch made history 'come alive' before the mind's eye. Thus, by reason of his engaging way of presenting the panorama of modern European history, my attention and predilection were gradually turned toward history to the exclusion of any other discipline. By the end of my senior year, therefore, the die had been cast in Clio's favor. That fact became unmistakably clear in the spring of 1927, when four of our class began serious preparation for taking the examinations for a Knights of Columbus

Fellowship at the Catholic University of America. In those examinations my major emphasis was on history not English. I shall treat the sequel to that examination in due course.

I trust that I have given proper credit to Father Lynch for the debt I owed to him. It was altogether real, even if I did discover during the early months of my graduate study that the notes taken in his history course were riddled with errors of fact. Having had no formal training in history would, I suppose, account in part for his indifference to accuracy, a price that had to be paid for the breezy lectures. In any case, I overcame the handicap in time and I remain to this distant day more than sixty years later thankful to this inspiring teacher who in 1933 joined the faculty of Chestnut Hill College in Philadelphia where he taught English until his death in October, 1963, at the age of sixty-nine.[3]

Let me turn now to the influence on my historical training of Edward Cardinal with a concluding note on another Saint Viator professor, Monsignor Gerasime M. Legris (1859-1934). First a few words about the college faculty in general. Like all other faculties Saint Viator had its share of the dull, the incompetent, and the indifferent; but it also had a number of gifted minds from whose instruction I profited, for example, John W.R. Maguire, C.S.V. (1883-1940) whose stimulating lectures in sociology and economics were quite above the average. I first came to know Ed Cardinal in my senior year when I enrolled in his course in historical method. This tall, good looking priest was then in his late twenties, having recently earned his master's degree in history at the Catholic University of America. If he lacked the rhetorical flourish and flair of Tom Lynch, he balanced his class presentation with a more critical approach, with an unceasing

---

[3]For furnishing data on Thomas Lynch I am indebted to Sister Consuelo Maria Aherne of Chestnut Hill College, Philadelphia, and Father Bernard G. Mulvaney, C.S.V., archivist of the Clerics of Saint Viator.

search for the root and cause of historical phenomena, and with a constant probing of students' minds by sharp questioning. I little realized then that this man of gracious manner and winning personality would in time become one of my closest priest friends, and that our correspondence which began after I left Bourbonnais would extend on for over a half century. And least of all did I realize that all the while he was saving my letters, a collection of about 700, which he had xeroxed and sent to me in the 1960's when he heard I was thinking of writing my memoirs.

Ed Cardinal was an ardent sports fan, an interest I did not share, but the time he gave to sports was never allowed to crowd out his zeal for reading. Few persons of my acquaintance kept more closely abreast of new publications—biographies, novels, short stories, and lengthy and solid histories. Here his influence on my academic life was in every sense helpful in directing my attention to areas of history where I was weak. After I received my doctorate in 1930 I was hired to teach history at Saint Viator and this gave Ed a chance to resume his graduate work at the University of Illinois where he took his Ph.D. degree in 1932 with a dissertation entitled, *Cardinal Lorenzo Campeggio, Legate to the Courts of Henry VIII and Charles V* (Boston, 1935).

Before leaving the subject of my college days I want to say something about the first monsignor whom I ever met, Gerasime M. Legris, ordained on his own patrimony, a venerable figure with white hair reaching to his shoulders, and one of the holiest persons I have ever known. Born into Bourbonnais' most prominent family of French Canadian background, he was a natural born aristocrat, exquisitely mannered, learned and well read. The course that I took from him, one I shall always remember, was the philosophy of history, about the nearest I came in college to what would today be called 'western civilization.' Our textbook was an abridged edition of the work of the Spanish priest-philosopher, Jaime Balmes (1810-1848), which was more a treatise in Catholic apologetics than an objective history. The monsignor made no pretense at being a scientific historian, and yet his stately demeanor, his carefully prepared lectures, and the force of his striking personality left a lasting impression on all of us. He had a profound love for France and a deep sympathy for the abbé Félicité de Lamennais (1782-1854) whose ideological differences with the Roman Curia and ultimate alienation from the Church saddened our old professor. Over a half century later I can still hear him closing his lecture on that subject with the words, "Poor Lamennais! Poor Lamennais!" It was a privilege to have known this elderly churchman, even if the inspiration of his personal example and virtue outweighed the benefit derived from his lectures in the philosophy of history. There are in life considerations that rise above that of the strictly academic achievement, considerations that relate to what is called character. In that regard Monsignor Legris stood tall in my mind, as I think he did in the minds of all who knew him.

One of the aspects of my formation as an historian was the acquiring at an early age of a love for reading. Had my father been an educated man, he would, as I suspect and have intimated, been a serious reader. Perhaps my own interest in that regard was due in part to an inherited characteristic. In any case, this feature of my intellectual training was given strong stimulation in college by the amount of reading assigned by professors like Tom Lynch. Moreover, it was the example of men like Lynch, Cardinal, and Legris that proved helpful in hearing them discuss books they were reading which, in turn, quickened my resolve to do likewise. To be sure, my reading tastes were not always those that would meet the approval of the so-called scientific historian. For example, I devoured the biographies of Hilaire Belloc whose writing style was truly superb, even if his fidelity to historical facts and his at times woefully biased interpretations left much to be desired. Yet once having acquired the taste, so to speak, I made gradual inroads on more substantial works. I can recall my curiosity being aroused about certain medieval popes to the point of seeking permission to sample Leopold von Ranke's *History of the Popes,* then on the Index of Forbidden Books and safely locked away behind a screened cabinet in the college library which, if I recall rightly, was termed 'little hell.' Graduate studies brought a wider approach when the Russian-born Michael Rostovtzeff's scholarly volumes on the social and economic history of the Roman Empire and of the Hellenistic world enriched my knowledge of ancient history, in the same way that Sidney Bradshaw Fay's two-volume masterpiece, *Origins of the World War* (1928), held me fascinated for days at a time, as with Fay's expert guidance I moved through the intricate diplomacy of the early twentieth century.

I have always been grateful to those who helped me acquire this habit of a lifetime. As I have told my students year in and year out there is no other road to travel if one is to learn history other than to read. It has not only furnished me with the best single avenue for learning what I have been called on to teach; it has done more, namely, afforded me some of the most pleasurable hours of my life. Never having developed hobbies or been absorbed in sports, reading has served to fill the time that others spend in those occupations. If I have at times carried the habit almost to excess, as my mother and my brother on occasion reminded me, I can honestly say I have found great personal enrichment in reading history. In fact, it has colored my mind and balanced my judgment as no other single factor save my religious faith. Moreover, it has saved me from more than one unthinking stance prompted by personal prejudice or the temptation to follow the crowd in joining a passing fad. In that sense my reading of history had done for me what Owen Chadwick meant when in his inaugural lecture as Regius professor of modern history at

Cambridge in 1968, he declared, "History. . . . does more than any other discipline to free the mind from the tyranny of present opinion."[4]

In listing certain factors that have a significant bearing on one's future life, Newman, as we have seen, maintained that as one looked back upon his or her past they would find how critical had been 'moments and acts,' among which were the 'accidents' that had determined a person's calling or prospects. I experienced such an 'accident' in the summer of 1927. As previously mentioned, four of our college class of that year took the examinations for a Knights of Columbus Fellowship, but no one of us emerged a winner. My initial failure prompted me to try to devise some way that I could go on to graduate study at the University of Illinois or elsewhere. I was getting nowhere with these plans when suddenly in July there arrived a letter from the Catholic University of America stating that one of the winners had dropped out and thus created a vacancy. Would I be interested? I lost no time in telegraphing my acceptance, a decision which was probably the most fateful for my future as an historian as any I have made before or since.

Frankly, I should have preferred to have taken my doctorate at one of the more prestigious universities if they would have accepted me. That, however, was out of the question, for although this was more than two years before the Great Depression struck in October, 1929, even then my father's hardware business was at a low ebb and he would have been unable to finance my graduate studies. Matters became a great deal worse, of course, after the collapse of the stock market in 1929, the effects of which I felt through my time in graduate school and well beyond. In other words, it was the Catholic University of America or nothing, and I gladly—and, I hope, gratefully—seized the opportunity.

---

[4]Owen Chadwick, *Freedom and the Historian. An Inaugural Lecture* (Cambridge, 1969) 39.

The Catholic University of America which I entered in September, 1927, was a far different institution that it is today. The enrollment of 892 students was hardly more than that of a fair sized college, the total endowment and annuity funds amounted at the end of my first year to $3,196,481, and the annual collection taken up throughout the parishes of the United States since 1904 and constituting one of the basic sources of income, yielded in 1928 the sum of $282,082.[5] It was little wonder that the university found it nigh to impossible to come abreast of its fellow members of the Association of American Universities to which it had been admitted as a charter member in 1900. The University's lack of an adequate endowment has been a crippling factor through its nearly 100 years of existence, a fact that has accounted in no small measure for its failure to achieve more significant results in the world of scholarship.

Be that as it may, the fellowship gave me a chance to pursue graduate studies, to say nothing of enlarging immensely my outlook on life with the national capital's numerous cultural advantages such as easy access to the incomparable resources of the Library of Congress to mention only a single example. It is not difficult to imagine what this meant to a recent college graduate, then age twenty-two, who had never before been east of Chicago. Upon arrival I turned to the only person in the university whom I had previously met, namely, Father Charles A. Hart (1893-1959), then an instructor in philosophy who had been born and raised in Ottawa, Illinois, twelve miles to the west of Seneca. A priest of the Diocese of Peoria, he had come to Washington after his ordination in 1919, began teaching philosophy in 1921, and continued on in that capacity until his death, having meanwhile earned the reputation of being

---

[5]For the data on the university in 1927-1928, see Note 14 of my essay, "The Catholic University of America, 1927-1979: A Personal Memoir," *Social Thought* 5 (Spring, 1979), 60.

the best professor in the School of Philosophy. When I inquired about the people in the Department of History, Charlie, as I came to call him, recommended that I major under Peter Guilday (1884-1947).

At the time Guilday, a priest of the Archdiocese of Philadelphia, forty-three years of age, was at his peak with a two-volume biography of Archbishop John Carroll (1922) and several other books to his credit, and before 1927 had run its course there appeared in two large volumes what was probably his best work, *The Life and Times of John England, First Bishop of Charleston, 1786-1842*. Trained under Alfred Cauchie (1860-1922) at the Catholic University of Louvain, Guilday's graduate work was in medieval and early modern ecclesiastical history with a doctoral dissertation entitled *The English Colleges and Convents in the Catholic Low Countries, 1558-1795* (1914). At our initial meeting he was courteous, although, I thought, somewhat reluctant to admitting a layman to a course and seminar composed predominantly of priests and nuns. But the hesitation, whether real or imagined on my part, soon gave way to a cordial reception which endured for the next twenty years until his death in July, 1947.

This was a time before the advent to the university faculty of the well trained and highly competent medievalist, Aloysius K. Ziegler (1895-1979). Peter had upon his coming to Washington in 1914 followed the advice of the university rector, Thomas J. Shahan (1857-1932), himself a church historian, and switched to the field of American Catholic history. He supplemented his work in that field, however, by lectures in medieval history. Precisely what motivated me in choosing the latter rather than the former, I cannot now recall. In any case, my major was in medieval history with the master's thesis, "Anti-Papal Legislation in Medieval England, 1066-1377," (1928) which was later expanded into the doctoral dissertation with the Ph.D. degree conferred in June, 1930, with Charlie Hart and Al Ziegler taking their doctorates at the same commencement. Like my mentor before me I switched fields twice before ultimately arriving at American Catholic history where I have remained since 1941.

With minor fields in the history of education and philosophy, the latter courses taken with Fulton J. Sheen (1895-1979), I took a variety of courses in history. All things considered, the most rewarding were those in ancient history with Martin R.P. McGuire (1897-1969), one of the most learned persons I have ever known, a man who left a deep imprint on my life as teacher, friend, and exemplar of a true Christian gentleman. Not only was I indebted to him for introducing me to the history of the ancient world in a thoroughly professional way but, too, for tutoring me in German, and enriching my intellectual life in any number of ways, not the least of which was the striking example he gave of high dedication to his vocation as a scholar. Martin later encouraged me in a number of enterprises, was a strong support as associate editor of the *Catholic Historical Review* during my years as editor, and was the *causa agitans* for the five articles I wrote for the *New Catholic Encyclopedia* (1967) of which his was the true guiding hand.

As for the minor fields, the lectures of Fulton Sheen were lively and held one's interest, even though my peculiarly factual mind left little doubt that I was not meant to be a philosopher. The two professors in the history of education conducted their classes in a mechanical and lifeless way that made no provision for questioning or discussion and I parted company with them with no regret. In the major field of history I supplemented Guilday's 'medieval institutions' with courses in modern European and American history. I wish that I could say that these courses measured up to those of Martin McGuire in ancient history, but in honesty I cannot. Nicholas A. Weber, S.M. (1876-1969), a genial and kindly man, was other than inspiring in European history, and we plodded through in a routine way that left no lasting imprint. The teachers in American history, Charles Hallan McCarthy

(1860-1941) and Richard J. Purcell (1888-1950), were well trained, the former having been a student of John Bach McMaster at the University of Pennsylvania where he earned his doctorate, and the latter took his Ph.D. at the University of Minnesota.

Perhaps McCarthy's age—he was then nearing seventy—prevented him from being a more effective instructor. A stately person who wore a high stiff collar and pince-nez glasses, he periodically conducted oral quizzes about the students' reading. "What are you reading?" he would ask. At least it was an invitation to read, even if there was no follow up on the question. During one of these sessions I remember a student replying that he was reading Guilday's biography of Archbishop Carroll, whereupon the old gentleman quietly commented, "Oh, yes, I taught him most of the English grammar he knows at Roman Catholic High School in Philadelphia some thirty years ago." He was given to piquant remarks of this kind which we often found amusing. The Minnesota man was unquestionably bright and knowledgeable, but a deep sense of grievance against the university for what he regarded as its unfair treatment and lack of recognition of him left a scar that had an adverse effect on his teaching. He was far outdistanced by Guilday in publications and reputation, a fact he seemed to resent. At times this sentiment spilled over to Guilday's students, as I personally experienced on occasion, for example, years later when he mercilessly quizzed Henry J. Browne (1919-1980), my doctoral candidate, to the point of causing this tough-minded New Yorker to weep after his final oral doctoral examination.

Accustomed as I had been to learning history through the medium of class lectures, I was not prepared for the approach of my major professor, Peter Guilday. He reflected his Louvain training in that he gave relatively little content in his classes. Elaborate schema or outlines were frequently passed out to us, but there followed no fleshing of the framework, so to speak. He had the gift, however, of arousing students' interest in church history, and of helping to sustain that interest through his up-to-date knowledge of new books and pertinent items from periodical literature. His personal relationship with students was invariably cordial, at times indulging them almost to a fault. If I did not derive content knowledge from his courses, I did profit for my entire lifetime from the stimulation he offered and the enthusiasm that he aroused in me and others for the history of the Church.

Guilday was a strikingly good looking man with a genuine flair for public address that brought him numerous invitations to speak. When I think of his faults—what one of us is free of them?—I am reminded of the remark made by a reviewer of the memoirs of Lauren Becall, the actress, who stated, "The most satisfying quality of this memoir is its generosity. . . . For her fellow performers there is virtually nothing but praise."[6] The same can be said of the more recent (1985) memoir of Sir Alec Guinness, *Blessings in Disguise.* In my effort to be objective I do not want to lose sight of that admirable quality. In the mind of one man I did just that when I devoted my Catholic Daughters of the Americas annual lecture to a memoir on my experience in the Catholic University of America in which I spoke of some of Guilday's weaknesses and received a scolding letter berating me for defaming a man no longer able to defend himself. That Peter was a complex character whose ambivalent stands at times left others bewildered, there is no doubt. That fact was evident in the 1985 essay of David J. O'Brien, "Peter Guilday: The Catholic Intellectual in the Post-Modernist Church."[7] I suppose every writer of a memoir can take

---

[6]Review of *Lauren Becall By Myself* (New York, 1979) by Larry McMurtry in the *New York Times Book Review,* January 7, 1979, p. 7.

[7]David J. O'Brien, "Peter Guilday: The Catholic Intellectual in the Post-Modernist Church," Nelson H. Minnich, Robert B. Eno, S S., and Robert Trisco (Eds.), *Studies in Catholic History In Honor of John Tracy Ellis* (Wilmington, Delaware, 1985) 260-306.

consolation—and refuge—in the remark of James Boswell in dedicating his famous biography of Samuel Johnson to Sir Joshua Reynolds, the distinguished portrait painter. Boswell declared: "Though I tell nothing but the truth, I have still kept in my mind that the whole truth is not always to be exposed."[8] The late Archbishop of Westminster, John Cardinal Heenan, put it another way when in 1971 he entitled the first volume of his memoirs, *Not The Whole Truth.*

Lest my remarks about Peter Guilday should cause anyone to wonder if he had been guilty of grave sins against his contemporaries, let it be said he had done nothing of the kind. If at times he left me wondering how to interpret his words and actions, he likewise left me with an abiding love of the history of the Church, and he furnished me and his other students with the tools of the trade so that we could make our own way after leaving his tutelage. That was much and for that I have always been grateful to him, as I was in 1939 when he brought me to the editorial board of the *Catholic Historical Review,* an experience that increased enormously my knowledge and my professional competence.

In regard to Monsignor Guilday *et al.,* I have been helped immensely in recalling persons and events by my correspondence, especially with the letters written to Ed Cardinal to which I have made reference. In fact, these letters at times revealed more about myself than I should care to know. Unlike Lauren Becall and Sir Alec Guinness, I found that on occasion I was anything but generous toward my contemporaries, but as Pilate once said, "What I have written, I have written," and I must abide by the record. One's letters may at times be the source of embarrassment, but they are likewise, all things considered, about as faithful a record of a person's mind as can be had. As the

---

[8]James Boswell, *The Life of Samuel Johnson,* abridged by Edmund Fuller (New York, 1960) 9. The dedication was dated at London, April 20, 1791.

distinguished English Benedictine historian David Knowles (1896-1974) maintained:

> Letters—a numerous and varied collection of letters—are the best of all mirrors of a man's character and mind and motives, whether he be a Cicero or a Bernard.[9]

In any case, early in life I acquired a penchant, as one of my church historian friends termed it, for correspondence. It has stood me in good stead, particularly when several of those to whom I wrote with regularity later returned my letters.

But I am straying. It is time to return to the business at hand and bring to a conclusion the account of my formal academic training. Obviously, one's professors and their classes are not the whole story in the making of an historian. There was also the experience of doing extended research projects. My first efforts in this area were under the direction of Peter Guilday who suggested that I write my master's thesis on the evolution of the *praemunire* statutes in Norman England. The thesis I wrote on this topic in 1928 was expanded into a doctoral dissertation which I published as my first book in 1930 under the title *Anti-Papal Legislation in Medieval England (1066-1377)*. I was not enthused by this topic but worked at it to the best of my abilities, doing what I was told to do. In the process, however, I lost any interest in doing further research in medieval history. When my first teaching assignments brought me into greater familiarity with the modern period, I welcomed the shift to this new area of research.

The other major factors shaping me as an historian during those years of graduate study were what one may call the environmental influences, and here the city of Washington and the surrounding area were rich in historical associations,

---

[9]David Knowles, *Saints and Scholars. Twenty-five Medieval Portraits* (Cambridge, 1962) 54.

buildings, and sites, such as the White House and Mount Vernon to name only two. My tours of these spots, my visits to the art galleries—the National Gallery of Art had not yet become a reality during my time in graduate school—and research institutions, such as the Library of Congress, were all of assistance in deepening and expanding my knowledge and in preparing me for my role as a teacher of history. Washington's great advantage in that regard was sharply etched in my mind when I left the capital in June, 1930, with my doctor's degree and began my teaching that summer at Saint Benedict's College in Atchison, Kansas, to be followed by four years of instruction, first at Saint Viator College (1930-1932) and then at the College of Saint Teresa (1932-1934) with the summers of 1933-1934 spent at Dominican College in San Rafael, California.

At all of these institutions I was made to feel welcome and efforts were made to make my time there pleasant and agreeable. In no single instance, however, was there any chance to specialize, for as I used to say, in these small liberal arts colleges I was asked to teach everything from 'the Hittites to Franklin D. Roosevelt.' Yet it had the advantage of forcing me to become acquainted with a broad spectrum of history—both secular and ecclesiastical—in a way that has proved advantageous for life, for there is no more effective way to learn any discipline than to attempt to teach it. I do not now recall any intention during those years to do research or serious writing beyond several popular articles. Even if I had been so disposed, the limited library facilities, the concentration on undergraduate instruction with large classes—there were over 100, mostly women religious, in Atchison—would render the possibility of such remote at best.

As in every aspect of life I experienced some disappointment and disillusionment during the early 1930's. It was in one of these colleges that I encountered for the first time on a broad scale cheating in examinations, and this in a class of predominantly women religious. It was an unpleasant discovery for a young layman who had been accustomed to putting trust in all that the sisters said and did. But there were compensating features as well, one of the most stimulating and satisfying of which in each of these colleges were a few very bright students. It was a joy to come in contact with these young and agile minds eager to learn. At Saint Viator, for example, there was Mary Cruise, a freshman from the neighboring town of Kankakee, one of the early girl students at the college. It was doubtless vanity that prompted me to save a letter that Mary wrote shortly after I left Bourbonnais in June, 1932. She had taken my course in the history of Greece and Rome, and after describing certain materials we had covered in class, she then said:

> All these things have lived and glowed and pulsated in our history classroom; it is no small tribute that men who have been dead twenty centuries and more have come alive at your touch, and that scenes which occurred when Parthenon and Capitol were young have become as much a part of reality as the events of our daily life. The great panorama has been unrolled for us, and we have been enriched with history, not merely taught it.[10]

I confess that my spirits were lifted by this unsolicited message from one of the ablest students I have had the privilege of teaching. It made the struggle to impart a knowledge of the ancient world, a field in which I was anything but a specialist, worth the effort.

In trying to appraise the circumstances that helped to shape my formation as an historian there was, as is true of every human being, the cultural factor. Having been born of a father of English Protestant background and a mother of

---

[10]Mary Cruise to John Tracy Ellis, Kankakee, Illinois, June 6, 1932.

Irish Catholic ancestry, that dual strain had its effect in coloring my outlook on life. While my brother and I were raised as Catholics from birth, our paternal inheritance made us at least aware of another religious tradition within our family circle. That awareness, however, was kept within certain limits, a point I have more than once illustrated by stating that during the time that my Grandmother Ellis, a devout Methodist, lived with us my mother would say on Sunday morning, "It is time for you to drive your grandmother to church, but don't go beyond the door." Mother would often attend Methodist suppers and social events, but religious services were quite another matter.

Although I never consciously assessed these home influences upon my role as an historian, in all likelihood they played their part in a subtle way. As for the spirit and temper of the Catholicism of my childhood and young manhood, it was what today would be termed the 'triumphalist church.' Allowing for one or two exceptions, my associates were predominantly Catholics from those in elementary school at Saint Patrick's in Seneca on through high school, college, and university. Were I to try to identify the triumphalist Church of my early years, I doubt that I could think of a more striking example than my enthusiastic participation in Chicago's International Eucharistic Congress in June, 1926, at the end of my junior year in college. I was there in Soldiers' Field on that memorable Holy Name Night when 100,000 men assembled with candles in hand for a ceremony presided over by the papal legate, Giovanni Cardinal Bonzano (1867-1927), in company with a dozen or more members of the College of Cardinals and, of course, the congress' host, George Cardinal Mundelein (1872-1939), Archbishop of Chicago, obviously bursting with pride at the stunning success of the event. For four days we followed the elaborate program that culminated at the archdiocesan seminary forty miles from the city where the alleged one million in attendance got thoroughly drenched in the downpour that came as the great procession of prelates was winding its way around the artificial lake. Neither before nor since have I experienced a dampening like unto it.

The psychology that accompanied the congress of 1926 would be all but incomprehensible to the Catholics of the 1980's. It must be remembered that the event occurred between the revival of the Ku Klux Klan (1915) and the launching of Protestants and Other Americans United for Separation of Church and State (1947). In other words, the organized anti-Catholic movement was then very much alive, a further factor in conditioning our thinking. That would account for the ghetto mentality that then prevailed among most American Catholics, and that was why they swelled with pride at the dazzling events of the Chicago congress. The latter took place two years before the ignominious defeat of Alfred E. Smith in the presidential compaign which scarred the American Catholic psyche for a decade or longer. In the political arena we Catholics of that era clung in the main to the Democratic Party as more friendly to the Church and to our immigrant heritage. In that regard our home was clearly divided with my father's adherence to the Republicans and me following my mother in her allegiance to the Democrats.

Still another influence that played its part in shaping my mind as an historian was travel. Thus my first trip to Europe in the summer of 1931, while I was still teaching mainly modern European history, was wonderfully enriching. Today trips of that kind have become so much a commonplace in the lives of Americans that to rehearse that trip in any detail would be both tedious and without point. Let me simply say that my two weeks in Spain with the following weeks in southern France, Switzerland, Italy as far as Rome, then into Germany, through Belgium to Paris, and finally to England and Ireland did more to enliven my lectures in the medieval and modern periods than anything I had experienced to date. One need only call the roll of certain places visited to know what is meant. For example, how better convey to the mind the somber character of Philip II of Spain than to stand before the fascade of El Escorial and to visit the royal tombs therein? In the same way, nowhere can one envision the power and affluence of the medieval papacy outside Rome itself than at the Palace of the Popes in Avignon, nor does the magnificence of the reign of Louis XIV come through anywhere quite like Versailles, nor the supreme artistry of medieval architecture than in the cathedral of Chartres. The same was true even to a greater degree in Rome, Munich, Cologne, Paris, London, and Dublin. I carried home not only postcards and pictures of these famous spots but as well mental pictures of Rome's splendors, of Cologne's majestic cathedral seen from the Rhine steamboat, of Les Invalides with its awesome tomb of Napoleon *et al.*, to say nothing of Les Carmes with its gruesome memories of the Reign of Terror, of London's Lambeth Palace that brought memories of the visits of Cardinal Wolsey at the height of his power, of The Tower where Saints Thomas More and John Fisher were imprisoned, and of Ireland where Dublin Castle recalled the long English dominance and of the south of the Emerald Isle where the Rock of Cashel and the numerous monastic ruins called to mind an age when Church and State in Ireland experienced a happier time.

Mutatis mutandis, I could say the same for my American travels, especially the summers of 1933 and 1934 when I took various routes to California where the chain of Franciscan missions was, so to speak, the *pièce de résistance* of my tours of the Far West, little knowing at that time that I was to live thirteen years in San Francisco (1963-1976) during which I improved my knowledge by visits far and wide to such historic landmarks as the missions in and around San Antonio, Texas, and to the charming Mission of San Xavier del Bac outside Tucson, Arizona.

In the lives of most men and women there are years that constitute a sort of watershed, years that mark the ending of one phases of our lives and the beginning of a new phase. The year 1934 was such in my life. Ever since I was a child I had thought off and on of becoming a priest, but it was definitely 'off and on,' and I came to no definite decision. As the time neared for me to graduate from Saint Viator Academy in 1923 I came close to joining the Viatorians, the only religious congregation that I knew up to that time. But once again the decision was put off and I proceeded to go through four years of college, three years of graduate work, and, indeed, four years of college level teaching before making up my mind.

I was then living in the Diocese of Winona and teaching at the College of Saint Teresa. I did not know the Bishop of Peoria in whose diocese I had been born, and I was told that Cardinal Mundelein would not accept me for Chicago where I had worked in the summers during my college years since I had not gone through Quigley Preparatory Seminary. I turned then to Francis M. Kelly (1886-1950), Bishop of Winona, who agreed to adopt me for his diocese, it being understood that I would pay my own way through the seminary and that I would teach after ordination rather than engage in the parochial ministry. Briefly that was what made 1934 a turning point in my life as I left Winona, Minnesota, and prepared to enter the Sulpician Seminary (Theological College since 1940) in Washington were Bishop Kelly agreed that I should study theology. He offered to send me to the North American College in Rome, but since I had to earn money to keep Norbert, my brother, in college I declined the offer, much to the chagrin of my best priest friend in Winona, Joseph F. Hale (1906-1957), a Roman alumnus who found it hard to forgive me for passing up the opportunity. Henceforth I was to live on two levels, as it were, a not at all unusual situation, for as Peter Gay once remarked:

Man lives in several worlds at once, most notably in his private sphere, in the comparatively intimate realm of his craft, and in the wide public domain of his culture.[11]

---

[11]Peter Gay, "Style in History," *American Scholar* 43 (Spring, 1974), 231.

For the next four years my craft was confined in the main to my 'private sphere,' while the making of a priest took center stage in my life.

CHAPTER II

A New Outlook

In entitling this chapter 'A New Outlook,' I have had in mind the necessary change of emphasis and viewpoint that came with my decision to study for the priesthood. That decision certainly did not preclude a further pursuit of history, although for the next four years it had to be subordinated to my immediate obligation, namely, theological studies and all the activities associated with seminary life. Since I had a doctorate in church history, I was excused from the seminary course in that subject, then taught by John K. Cartwright (1893-1972), a self-taught but highly learned priest, with whom I was later to become a close friend. Perhaps the 'advanced' age of twenty-nine accounted for my being excused from Hebrew as well! In any case, the classes in theology, Scripture, canon law *et al.* allowed time to follow a course in elementary Italian at the university across the street from the seminary where Father Joseph P. Christopher (1890-1964), like myself from the Illinois River Valley (Peru), not only gave us a genuine feeling for that beautiful language—and for its proper pronunciation—but likewise entertained us no end with his daily witticisms. As was true of Cartwright, so after ordination I became a good friend of Chris, a learned classicist, from whose table conversation in Curely Hall I benefited for a decade or more.

If the years 1934-1938 did not mark any significant progress in my life as an historian, they yet afforded sufficient leisure for keeping reasonably abreast of new documentation, books, and periodical literature that came out at that time. And in that regard the resources of the university's Mullen Library, with occasional visits to the Library of Congress, proved beneficial. With the opening of the next academic year in September, 1935, several happenings served to deepen my historical sense and knowledge.

As previously mentioned, I had taught at the university's Pacific Coast Summer Session in San Rafael, California, in the summers of 1933 and 1934. There I came to know well the founder and director, James Marshall Campbell (1895-1977). And through Martin McGuire and Father Campbell, I became well acquainted with their colleague of the Department of Greek and Latin, Roy J. Deferrari (1890-1969), who as Dean of the Graduate School and holder of other high administrative offices, including the summer sessions, wielded a good deal of power under the current rector, James Hugh Ryan (1886-1947). It was through that chain of command, so to speak, that an added dimension emerged for me in a two-fold way. First, Deferrari asked Father Anthony Viéban, S.S. (1872-1944), rector of the seminary, if I might teach a course in undergraduate history in the College of Arts and Sciences. Having been assured that by reason of my having taught the course for four years and having it well enough in hand not to need a great amount of time to be taken from my theological studies, the rector gave his assent. Secondly, Deferrari asked me if I would assume the duties of director of a new branch summer session scheduled to open in San Antonio, Texas, that summer of 1935. In both cases the teaching of modern European history helped to solidify my knowledge by expanded reading in that highly important field.

If the three summers in San Antonio (1935-1937) added little to my knowledge of European history, they were of benefit in other respects. By side trips out of San Antonio, the most memorable being a train ride to Monterrey and Saltillo in Mexico, which was my first venture into Latin America, a region that up to that time was a *terra incognita* to this mid-westerner, I learned a good deal about our American Southwest and its distinctly Hispanic background. The post of director also taught me much about human nature. Fearing to offend either of the two Catholic colleges for women in San Antonio, the university divided the summer session between Our Lady of the Lake College and Incarnate Word College.

I lived at Our Lady of the Lake but made daily trips to Incarnate Word, not an enviable undertaking beneath the blazing Texas sun. Trying to keep the two rival institutions happy was at times like sailing between Scylla and Charybdis, and on occasion I was at my wits' end to know how to maintain the proper balance. In this sense the experience was enlightening as a laboratory in human relations. Having been informed in advance of the strong-minded dean of Our Lady of the Lake, Mother Angelique Ayers (1882-1968), I felt I had to hold my ground when she intervened to protest the grade of F given to several of the sisters of her community. I hope I did the latter no injustice in refusing to budge, for I reasoned that if I yielded to this plea I might well be lost should a similar encounter occur. Mother Angelique was an admirable woman, to be sure, one who went out of her way to make my stay pleasant, for example, initiating my trip to Mexico. All the same, I felt I had to make it clear from the outset who was running the summer session.

The second opening of 1935 proved to be much more significant for my future as an historian. I have always found the teaching of a new group of students both a challenging and an enriching experience. True, the majority of students usually pass in and out of one's classes and are heard of no more. But there are the exceptional cases where a teacher senses that he or she has been put in contact with young minds that offer great promise. Such was true of two in particular in that class of September, 1935, namely, Roland E. Murphy, O.Carm., and John K. Zeender. The former went on to become an internationally recognized authority in Old Testament studies, and the latter earned an enviable reputation as an outstanding teacher of modern German history after receiving his doctorate at Yale. And there were others besides Murphy and Zeender. Obviously, it is a risky business to single out special names from a large group, but I trust I shall not be thought guilty in that regard if I mention several others. For example, there was Humberto Medeiros (1915-1983), who died as Cardinal Archbishop of Boston, and his classmate and close friend, James D. Collins (1917-1985), whose numerous publications in the history of philosophy won him an international reputation. As undergraduates these two men used to write term papers the equal of some master's theses with citation of French and German sources. Still another, Leo Brady (1917-1984) acquired fame in his role as a playwright and professor of drama, and Timothy F. Lynch (1920-1985) earned high respect in the field of labor law. All these have since died, but Ernest L. Unterkoefler, Bishop of Charleston since 1964, continues to make his mark in the field of ecumenism, as has his classmate of 1940, James C. (Jay) Turner who for many years gave conspicuous leadership in the trade union world. There were others, to be sure, but let these names suffice to indicate the caliber of students whom I had the privilege of teaching as undergraduates between 1935 and 1942 when, as I shall explain, my life as a historian took another turn.

Upon my ordination to the priesthood on June 5, 1938, my first summer was given in the main to the parochial ministry at Saint John the Baptist Parish on West 50th Place in Chicago. That September I moved into the home of Fulton J.

Sheen, then a professor of philosophy in the university, whom I had served as secretary for several years while doing my graduate work. Residence on Cathedral Avenue, N.W., was a pleasant experience, although it neither added nor subtracted anything from my historical formation. More to the point, I began full time teaching in the Department of History that fall with the principal emphasis on modern Europe along with a survey course in American history for a group of soldiers who were soon to see action in World War II. While these courses were in secular history, my strong leaning toward church history found an outlet in my growing interest in the career of Pope Pius VII's Secretary of State, Ercole Cardinal Consalvi (1757-1824). I became fascinated by the famous papal diplomat and an original intention of writing an article gradually expanded to the proportions of a book as I gathered more material from the printed sources and secondary literature, along with an occasional item from the scholarly periodicals. From the outset I was conscious, needless to say, of the desirability of research in the Vatican Archives, but a combination of limited finance, the outbreak of war in September, 1939, and summer school obligations prevented me from undertaking research abroad. Meanwhile I kept working away and in 1942 the university press brought out my second book, *Cardinal Consalvi and Anglo-Papal Relations, 1814-1824,* which in spite of its lack of original sources in both Rome and London was reasonably well received and won for me a promotion to the rank of associate professor.

Apart from my long standing love of biography, perhaps my favorite mode of learning history, I was intrigued by Consalvi's extraordinary success in such delicate negotiations as those leading up to the signing of the concordat with Napoleon Bonaparte in July, 1801, and winning back the Papal States for Pius VII at the Congress of Vienna. True, the latter was achieved as part of the principle of restoring the legitimate prerevolutionary rulers to their thrones. All the same it was a notable achievement for a churchman to make that progress in a thoroughly secular setting. The cardinal was anything but a real liberal by nineteenth-century standards, but he was head and shoulders above his fellow members of the College of Cardinals in the recognition that the political world had profoundly changed and that the Church in consequence would have to adjust to that fact. Moreover, the man displayed character in his stubborn adherence to principle as he saw it, and that won my admiration. Even so constant an opponent as Bonaparte, with whom Consalvi sparred for months at a time, shared this opinion. For example, in their final strange encounter at Fréjus in the spring of 1814 when the fallen emperor's carriage stopped for overnight, Consalvi now liberated and on his way to join the pope at Cesena passed the same way. Seeing Consalvi standing on a bit of high ground while waiting for a change of horses, Napoleon remarked to Marshal von Keller sitting at his side, "He is a man who does not wish to appear to be a priest, but he is more a priest than all the rest of them."[1] Coming from Bonaparte, it was a high compliment, the kind of evidence that helped to quicken my interest in Consalvi's career.

One of the most helpful factors in rounding out my training as an historian came in February, 1939, with my appointment to the editorial board of the *Catholic Historical Review,* quarterly journal of the American Catholic Historical Association. My initial assignment was as editor of the book reviews, a task that gave me a close acquaintance with new publications in all aspects of ecclesiastical history from antiquity to the present. It likewise brought a broader knowledge of specialists in various fields as I searched out the best reviewers for incoming books. This assignment also put

---

[1] Fredrik K. Nielsen, *History of the Papacy in the XIXth Century* (New York, 1906) I, 338. Consalvi was ordained a deacon but was never a priest.

me in daily touch with older and more experienced historians such as Peter Guilday, Martin McGuire, and Aloysius Ziegler, to name only three of those with whom I served on the *Review's* board. I shall have occasion to mention my connection with the *Review* in what follows, but I wish to record here how greatly I was benefited by this editorial work all through the more than twenty-two years I served the journal to my resignation in December, 1962. In fact, after the teaching of history and research and writing it, I know of no better way to deepen one's knowledge and sharpen one's commitment to an academic discipline than to edit a scholarly journal dedicated to that discipline's advancement.

The year 1941 proved to be a pivotal one for me in more than one way. Monsignor Guilday's health had been deteriorating for some time by reason of diabetes, and the responsible persons in both the Association and the *Review* had—unknown to me—discussed the matter at a private gathering during the Association's annual meeting in New York in Christmas Week. As a consequence I was appointed acting secretary of the Association and managing editor of the *Review* in February, 1941, following Guilday's resignation of both offices. If the change increased my work there was compensation in reducing my teaching schedule which was soon standardized at one lecture course of three hours a week and a two-hour seminar.

An even more significant change came in July, 1941, when Bishop Joseph M. Corrigan (1879-1942), rector of the university, sent for me to ask if I would take over Peter Guilday's courses in American Catholic history. "I do not know anything about the field," I said, whereupon Corrigan replied, "You can learn, can't you?" I agreed I could do that if I were given time and the rector stated I would be given a year to prepare for this new field. I decided to devote the first semester to acquainting myself with the literature and started off with John Gilmary Shea's four-volume *History of the Catholic Church in the United States,* an old work that gave the most detailed account of Catholic developments down to the Second Plenary Council of Baltimore in 1866. It was far from the critical approach demanded at a later time, but it gave me at least a knowledge of the broad lines of the American Catholic story. I supplemented Shea with key biographies such as Guilday's two-volume lives of John Carroll and John England and other secondary works while I examined the few periodicals devoted to the field such as the *Saint Louis Catholic Historical Review,* the publications of the Catholic historical societies of Philadelphia and New York, and the back volumes of that superior journal of its time, the *American Catholic Quarterly Review* that had begun in 1876 and ceased publication in 1924. I soon became aware of the importance of the archives of the Archdiocese of Baltimore which I visited, taking notes but little realizing how much time I was to spend there from July, 1945, on for several years while doing research for the life of Cardinal Gibbons.

The first semester of my year's sabbatical thus passed swiftly, and by the opening of 1942 I had at least learned the essential facts of this new field and felt ready to embark on a more ambitious program by spending the second semester at Harvard where I decided to audit the courses of Arthur M. Schlesinger Sr. (1888-1965) and Frederick Merk (1887-1977) and avail myself of the riches of the Widener Library. I was fortunate in being invited to live at Saint Anthony Rectory in Allston by the pastor, John E. Sexton (1886-1949), former professor of church history in Saint John's Seminary, Brighton, and one of the authors of the three-volume work, *History of the Archdiocese of Boston* (1944). Johnny, as he was called, was a mine of information, as was Robert Howard Lord (1885-1954), who kindly put at my disposal certain works in the library of Saint John's Seminary where he was then a professor, works that I did not find at the Widener Library.

The 'Harvard interval,' as I have at times called it, was a period of genuine enrichment in more ways than one. From my initial contacts with Crane Brinton (1898-1968), then chairman of the Department of History, I had never before experienced such uniform courtesy as I met at Harvard, and that from administrators, faculty members, and students. I have always maintained that courtesy is closely related to good morals in the sense of showing consideration for others. In that regard the people I encountered at Harvard, and in 1967 at Brown when I was a visiting professor there, might well feel themselves remote from what Belloc had in mind in his little poem, yet his words might fittingly have been applied to them:

Of Courtesy, it is much less
Than courage of heart and holiness,
Yet in my walks it seems to me
That the grace of God is in Courtesy.

For obvious reasons I enrolled in the course of Arthur Schlesinger, Sr., a ranking authority in American social history, and in that of Frederick Merk whose specialty was the history of the American West. Samuel Eliot Morison (1887-1976) was at the time on leave, to my disappointment, for I should have liked to follow one or other of the classes of this notable scholar. Merk was a rather sober man whose classes were informative and well prepared, even if they did not answer to what has become a very tired word—'exciting.' I recall his saying to me at our first meeting, "I have a grudge against your Church for taking Bob Lord away from us." Lord had taught at Harvard for many years, served as chairman of the department, and was highly esteemed. He converted to Catholicism, decided to study for the priesthood, and was ordained in 1929.

My most memorable and profitable personal relationship at Harvard was, however, with the senior Schlesinger who with his charming wife, Elizabeth, would frequently entertain his graduate students at Sunday afternoon teas. These gatherings were noted for the openness and warmth that obtained when 'shop talk' was often supplemented by an exchange of views about current movements in both Church and State. I attended these sessions faithfully and found them enlightening, and with a single exception altogether pleasant. The exception related to the subject of Father Charles E. Coughlin (1891-1979) and his paper, *Social Justice.* I was queried as to the connection, stated quite accurately that I did not know what the relationship was, only to be charged by one guest as being "evasive." It was characteristic of Arthur Schlesinger that he should have come to me before class the next day, invited me to lunch in Adams House, and there told me he wished to apologize for the episode that had taken place in his home. I found it easy to agree with Henry May, himself an authority in the field, when a year before Schlesinger died he described him as "the best-informed and most influential student of American social history. . . ."[2]

My friendship with this urbane and gentle scholar and his wife was one of the most abiding and cherished memories of my time at Harvard. It led on one occasion to another embarrassment, this time of my own making. I was frequently quizzed by the Schlesingers and their friends about things Catholic, they confessing that they took the opportunity of speaking to a priest about aspects of Catholic life that had aroused their curiosity. In all likelihood stimulated by the current and growing vogue for the works of the Cistercian monk, Thomas Merton (1915-1968), I volunteered to drive them, and Richard Storr and his wife, a Schlesinger graduate student later on the faculty of York University in Ontario, to Valley Falls, Rhode Island, to visit the Trappist monastery located there. As it turned out

---

[2]Henry F. May, "The Recovery of American Religious History," *American Historical Review* LXX (October, 1964) 83.

Professor Schlesinger could not make the trip, but Elizabeth Schlesinger and the Storrs were present, only for me to be told by the guest master that Dick and I might be shown through the monastary, but not the two ladies. I was deeply embarrassed at having to leave them in the vestibule of the monastic church while we toured the interior in silence. I recall Dick's amusement in reading a notice on one of the bulletin boards as we passed along the corridor: "Will the Brother, who borrowed my copy of the *Imitation of Christ,* please return it." The Trappist rule of the early 1940's was stricter than it is today, and I should have known better than to invite two ladies to see Saint Joseph's before making inquiry concerning the rules governing visitors. It was in good measure a lost afternoon for them, but they took it good naturedly as we drove back to Cambridge.

As I glance back over the more than sixty years since I first embarked on my training as an historian, I can honestly apply to myself the words of Nicholas Murray Butler (1862-1947), the longtime President of Columbia University, who described himself in his memoirs as, "one who has had and is having the inestimable pleasure and satisfaction of a busy, an interesting and a happy life. . . ."[3] In examining the galaxy of famous names that adorn the Butler memoirs, however, I quickly realized what an immense gap there was between him and me in the number and variety of famous people who had crossed our paths. I am prompted to mention that at this point, since at Harvard—thanks largely to Crane Brinton—I met more persons of fame than I had before or since. In that regard I have been relatively immune from what Robert Speaight once contended was an attribute of those who wrote their memoirs. "The art of autobiography," he declared, "—it must be confessed—lies

---

[3]Nicholas Murray Butler, *Across the Busy Years. Recollections and Reflections* (New York, 1935) 1.

partly in dropping the right names in the right places. . . ."[4]
If that be true, one of the few times in my life when that
offered a threat were the months spent in Cambridge where
those famous in the academic and cultural world were and
are in ample supply.

That proved to be especially true the night that Crane
Brinton invited me to be his guest at the annual dinner for the
Society of Fellows, a handpicked group of promising young
men chosen to enable them to do research with the specific
provision that they not work for degrees. Among the twenty
some fellows on that occasion were two Catholics, one of
Polish descent and one of Irish descent. In the distinguished
company that evening was the venerable A. Lawrence Lowell
(1856-1943), a political scientist best known for his nearly
quarter century as President of Harvard. Sitting close by was
Alfred North Whitehead (1861-1947), a world renowned
philosopher, and the historian of ancient religions, Arthur
Darby Nock (1902-1963), at the time editor of the *Harvard
Theological Review*. When Nock learned that I was from the
Catholic University of America, I thought he was going to
embrace me so enthused did he become by reason of the
university having, as he said, "brought that great scholar,
Johannes Quasten (1900-1987) to this country." Given my
lifelong dedication to John Henry Newman, I must have
caught my breath when Whitehead informed me that he
believed he was one of the few living persons who had
lunched with Cardinal Newman!

During my conversation with Mr. Lowell, the old
gentleman reminisced in a manner appropriate to one of so
impeccable a Brahmin background, dropping a few names on
his own as he chatted on about his acquaintance with
Woodrow Wilson, Cardinal Mercier *et al.* At one point he
remarked, "Years ago we wanted to give one of your

---

[4]Review of Harold Acton, *More Memoirs of An Aesthete* (London,
1970) by Robert Speaight in *The Tablet* (London) 224 (May 9, 1970) 451.

professors of church history (I do not recall his mentioning the name) an honorary degree; he refused, and it was not for a long time that we found out why—Cardinal O'Connell would not let him take it." I replied, "That feeling has now changed, I believe; it is water under the bridge," whereupon the octogenarian quietly commented, "Yes, and it was good water, for it purified the stream." I had been told that the cardinal's attitude toward Harvard had mellowed somewhat in recent years, perhaps not uninfluenced by the honorary degree that he himself was awarded there at the commencement of 1937.

When I think of the fact that I then thought it of worth to note the presence of the two Catholics among the Harvard Fellows, it brings to mind what an immense change there has been in that regard since 1942. The difference was highlighted for me in 1966 when H. Stuart Hughes, then a professor of history at Harvard, told my friend, John Whitney Evans of the College of Saint Scholastica, Duluth:

Before the war, Catholic graduate students in history at Harvard were few in number, mostly undistinguished, and on the margin of intellectual exchange; the rest of us treated them with politeness, but it would not have occurred to us to discuss religious or philosophical matters with them (and perhaps they themselves would have been embarrassed to do so.) Today my Catholic graduate students are some of the very best I have, they are right in the center of student life, and they do not hesitate to discuss the most prickly topics frankly and cordially.[5]

---

[5]H. Stuart Hughes to John Whitney Evans, Paris, November 4, 1966. I wish to thank both Professor Hughes and Father Evans for permission to quote this letter.

That change has continued to the present day, not only in the field of history but in other fields as well, for example, in theology where the divinity schools at Harvard, Yale, and Princeton have Catholics enrolled to nearly half of their student bodies. It was all a part of the maturing process of the erstwhile immigrant American Catholic community that has wrought so many and so varied alterations in that community since World War II.

As a priest-historian I have lived for a half century in two worlds, so to speak, the ecclesiastical and the academic. My primary motive in going to Harvard was to seek further knowledge and cultivation in history. But all the while I was daily immersed in the ecclesiastical in the company of fellow priests at Saint Anthony's Parish and in Boston generally, offering Mass and hearing confessions and preaching which I gladly did to help compensate for my board and room since the pastor would not hear of my paying for my lodging and food. These were the closing years of that formidable churchman, William Cardinal O'Connell (1859-1944) who had ruled the Archdiocese of Boston since 1907. Formidable he certainly was, as I was to learn in more ways than one, for example, when a Sister of Notre Dame de Namur at Emmanuel College, whom I had taught at Washington, asked me to lecture at Emmanuel, an invitation I accepted only to be told that the archdiocesan chancery had declined permission when my former student applied there. No reason was given, and to this day I have remained in the dark about the matter. It was not without precedent, for some years before when the distinguished Belgian historian of medieval philosophy, Maurice de Wulf (1867-1947), of the Catholic University of Louvain, was invited to lecture at Harvard, O'Connell ordered that he not be given faculties to offer Mass, not knowing that de Wulf was a married layman with several children.

Since I had been asked to teach American Catholic history, it occurred to me that something might be gained by my becoming acquainted with those who had made that history. I inquired of the priests at Saint Anthony's and they assured me that if I applied for an interview with Cardinal O'Connell it would be granted. It turned out just as they had predicted and I was promptly informed by the chancery that I should present myself on a particular March morning. I was not kept waiting very long before I was summoned to the cardinal's office where I found the old churchman, then eighty-three and partially blind, sitting behind the desk with his faithful black poodle dog, Moro, seated at his feet. The hand was held forth for me to kiss the cardinal's ring, whereupon he bid me welcome and beckoned me to sit on the backless bench in front of his desk.

The cardinal's moods seemed to be registered in the rise and fall of his rich metallic voice, starting off rather softly in saying I was welcome and then the voice rising as he cautioned me, "Remember, Father, you are a priest first; don't try to be a Harvard man!" Having been informed of why I had come to Harvard, he used most of the time in lecturing me on how he thought the history of the Church should be written. He was obviously irked by Theodore Maynard's recent book, *The Story of American Catholicism,* asked if I had read it, and learning that I had, he said, "What do you think of it?" I replied that I thought Maynard had handled two of the most difficult topics quite well. "What were they?" he asked. I answered trusteeism and Americanism. To that the cardinal raised his voice and declared, " I don't think any of it was well done. I don't think the book should have ever been written. Do you have to go to the backhouse to get history?" He then continued that I should remember that the Church was a sacred thing, that it was the bride of Christ, and its history should be treated reverently. Several times the cardinal admonished me, "Remember, you are in a position to do something about it," to all of which I listened in silence, sensing the depth of his ire and realizing that I could do little to change his mind. The discourse went on for about twenty minutes or a half hour, and I then thinking that I had taken his measure to some degree, stated that I did not wish to encroach upon his time. He quickly made it known that he still had a few things left to say by replying, "Just a minute, Father, just a minute." The implication was clear: he would dismiss me, I would not dismiss myself. After a few more cautions about how to treat the history of the Church—such a thing as a critical approach would have been out of the question—he signaled that the interview was ended by holding his hand aloft for the ring to be kissed once again, wished me well, and assured me as I moved toward the door that they would do all they could to make my stay pleasant—with a final reiteration, "Remember, you are in a position to do something about it."

As I drove back to Allston late that morning, I pondered over what had so roused the old man's indignation in Maynard's book. Upon reaching the rectory I took down my copy and wondered had I perhaps guessed the reason when I found O'Connell's name mentioned only once in the index in connection with his receiving the red hat in 1911, whereas there were two chapters entitled, "The Age of Gibbons," and "The Death of the American Cardinal." It was obvious that Gibbons was something of a hero to Maynard, and that might have been too much for Boston's first cardinal whose strong strain of personal vanity was well known. Yet another possible reason for his criticism of Maynard was the latter's sharp remarks about the role played by many of the Irish in the American Church, and this coming from a convert to Catholicism of English background may well have made it all the more offensive.[6]

The interview with Cardinal O'Connell proved enlightening for several reasons. It gave me first hand evidence of the spirit and tone in which he and many of the bishops of his

---

[6]For a more detailed account, see John Tracy Ellis, *Catholic Bishops: A Memoir* (Wilmington, 1984) the chapter entitled, "Most Fabulous Of All, William Cardinal O'Connell," pp. 67-77.

generation wished the history of the Church to be written. In fact, I would say that such was the attitude of a great majority of both bishops and priests who revealed the defensive reaction of men who had grown up in the aftermath of the A.P.A. and the decades of the flourishing Ku Klux Klan. In a word, such a thing as telling the Church's story in an open and honest way was giving consolation to the enemy. That attitude touched even the more enlightened among them, for example, Edward Cardinal Mooney (1882-1958), Archbishop of Detroit. When I visited Detroit while doing research for the life of Cardinal Gibbons he received me with genuine warmth and during lunch told stories about Bernard McQuaid, one of his predecessors as Bishop of Rochester, but with the caution, "Now don't put these into your next book." When I replied I had no intention of doing so, he rejoined, "I'm not sure. If you were like Reuben Parsons (who wrote 'pious' history), but you are one of these frank guys." That these bishops—and superiors of religious orders as well—impeded the writing of good history, there is no doubt. The examples could be multiplied but I will cite only one more here. Following the publication of my life of Gibbons I was told by several people that John J. Mitty (1884-1961), Archbishop of San Francisco, had said he was going to destroy all his papers so that "no one can do that to me," a threat which, fortunately, he never got around to carrying out, but Richard Cardinal Cushing (1895-1970), Archbishop of Boston, did just that, as did others, to the great loss of history. While fully conscious of the attitude of these churchmen, I never allowed it to influence my own writing of church history since I simply did not believe in the validity of their position. I have always preferred the attitude represented by Pope Leo XIII in his letter on historical studies of 1883 where he made his own the words of Job, "God has no need for our lies."[7]

---

[7]"Leo XIII on Ecclesiastical Studies," *Catholic University Bulletin* V (October, 1899) 494. The full text of the pope's letter is printed here (pp. 487-502).

Before concluding this account of my time at Harvard I wish to record two more related matters. At the time, the authors of the *History of the Archdiocese of Boston* were hard at work on the closing aspects of that ambitious undertaking. Johnny Sexton told me that the cardinal would say to them, "Hurry up! I want to see it before I die." Since he was paying for it all ($16,000, I was told), that was natural enough. Ironically, he died in April, 1944, only a few weeks before Sheed & Ward brought out the finished product. The three large volumes represented a real achievement with their thorough research, highly detailed treatment, and clear writing style. The second half of Volume III, however, was not history so much as hagiography, a section comprising over 330 printed pages that dealt with the regime of O'Connell. Among the sources cited at the outset was a work entitled, *The Letters of His Eminence William Cardinal O'Connell, Archbishop of Boston,* Volume I, *From College Days 1876 to Bishop of Portland 1901* (Cambridge: The Riverside Press, 1915). This 280-page work was purportedly a series of letters written between 1876 and 1901 to family and friends recounting O'Connell's experiences in detail.

I first became aware of this work when years ago a Boston priest told me about it and remarked, "My pastor and the cardinal's nephew spent an entire afternoon shoveling copies into the furnace." Not long after its appearance a Boston newspaper man set out to review it, became suspicious of its content, and let his suspicions be known, whereupon the destruction promptly ensued. The book had been written by O'Connell long years after the supposed date of the letters, and when its actual origin was discovered an effort was made to blot out all memory of the work. Some copies escaped, however, and nigh to a half century later I was shown a copy in the library of a southern diocese. I confess I was more shaken by finding it seriously cited by a church historian of Lord's background than I was by O'Connell's faked correspondence. I frequently took it to my seminar in later years to show my graduate students and to indicate the critical attitude an historian must always exercise toward the sources he or she employs in their work. One learns the rules of the game, so to speak, in more ways than one!

Let me recount one final aspect of my sojourn in New England before resuming the narrative in Washington. At the dinner for the Society of Fellows mentioned above I was seated at table next to Dr. Heinrich Breuning (1885-1970), former Chancellor of Germany in the days leading up to the Nazi takeover in 1933. Breuning like so many others was destined to be liquidated, but he made good his escape and came to the United States where the distinguished statesman was offered a position as professor of government at Harvard. Given his background he was understandably cautious with new acquaintances, and that added to his natural shyness made him something less then informative at our initial meeting, although unfailingly polite.

As the evening wore on, however, he warmed a bit and accepted my invitation to lunch at the Hotel Commander some blocks from Harvard Square. On this occasion Breuning was seemingly quite relaxed and we chatted amiably for an hour or more during which he told me that as chancellor he had sent to Rome numerous documents by way of warning Pope Pius XI of the Nazi peril, only to learn to his chagrin that they had never reached the pontiff. They were withheld, he said, by the Secretary of State, Eugenio Cardinal Pacelli, the future Pius XII. That Breuning still resented this action was plain as he related the incident with some animation peering through his thick glasses directly at me. For this relatively unenlightened young church historian it was a revealing episode, a minor one, to be sure, but one that lent an insight into the complicated world of ecclesiastical diplomacy.

The months spent at Harvard were a genuinely enriching experience. Not only did I deepen my knowledge of the American past with a special emphasis on its religious and social aspects, but I had the good fortune to meet and exchange ideas with experts in the field, and that was especially true of Arthur Schlesinger Sr., as well as the circle of bright young graduate students gathered about him. To most of them it was a novel experience to come to know a Catholic priest, and I was constantly pried with questions about the Church and her policies. Periodically I described my experiences to my friend, Ed Cardinal, who as I have said, saved all my letters and thus enabled me to recall many events with a precision that would otherwise be lacking.

My time in New England coincided with the early stages of active American involvement in World War II, and soon wartime restrictions were being felt on all sides in the shortage of gasoline, the difficulty to get new tires, etc. My Chevrolet served me well, however, although when a seminary classmate came along in the summer of 1942 and said he was in the market for a car I promptly sold him the Chevrolet and thereafter did not own an automobile. But owning or not owning an automobile has little to do with the making of an historian which is the principal focus of this memoir. More to the point, as I drove back to Washington in late May, 1942, I felt reasonably well prepared to begin my new assignment to teach American Catholic history.

CHAPTER III

Home At Last

When my colleague, Father Carlton M. Sage, S.S., heard I was about to publish a volume entitled *The Formative Years of the Catholic University of America* (1946), he asked, "Are you going to change your field now? Each time you have published a book you have made such a change." I replied that this time there would be no further change. With the history of American Catholicism I was 'home for good,' so to speak. In the more than forty years that have passed since that time I have had no inclination or desire to make another change since I have felt so much at home in this branch of history and have enjoyed the work beyond that of all my previous undertakings in Clio's name and company.

Succeeding Peter Guilday was no minor task, for in addition to his having founded the American Catholic Historical Association (1919) and edited its quarterly journal, he had an impressive record for both personal research and publication as well as for having directed thirty-three published doctoral dissertations. Peter was *facile princeps* among those who worked in this field as he bravely carried on the tradition of the founding father, John Gilmary Shea (1824-1892). Having spent the summer of 1942 in further reading, editing the *Review,* and conducting the business of the Association, I was ready to begin teaching in September.

Being a newcomer to the field I went to far greater detail in covering the colonial period than I would have done as a more experienced teacher of the subject. In fact, I spent most of the first year on the colonial period, but thereafter drastically cut it down so as to emphasize the far more important aspects of the Church's American story that began in 1790 with the episcopacy of John Carroll.

One of the most rewarding features of teaching American Catholic history was the direction of graduate students. They were never great in number, and with an exception or two were then all priests and women religious. There were some first class minds among them who proved to be highly stimulating for this newcomer who was then still relatively young at thirty-seven. My first doctoral student was inherited from Peter Guilday, namely, Hugh J. Nolan, like Guilday himself from the Archdiocese of Philadelphia who published a solid study of the Philadelphia episcopacy of Francis Patrick Kenrick (1948) and who has since edited a four-volume set of the pastoral letters of the American bishops while serving as pastor of Saint Isaac Jogues Parish at Wayne, Pennsylvania.

Five of my doctoral candidates of the late 1940's and 1950's are now dead: Patrick H. Ahern of the Archdiocese of Saint Paul, Henry J. Browne of the Archdiocese of New York, Sister Alphonsine Frawley of Regis College, Weston, Peter J. Rahill of the Archdiocese of Saint Louis, and Sister Hildegarde Yeager of Saint Mary's College, Notre Dame. Likewise deceased are two Benedictine monks who took their master's degree with me, Bosco Cestello of Saint Vincent Archabbey and Edmund Halsey of Saint Mark Priory in South Union, Kentucky, and there may, indeed, be others of whom I lost track.

I found in all these graduate students a stimulation as well as a challenge to keep a step ahead, or at least abreast, of their quick and inquiring minds. It was a joy to observe their intellectual development and to witness in later years how the creative spirit prompted a number of them to research and write books and articles of lasting value that advanced our knowledge of varying aspects of the American Catholic past. As I have said, mentioning names is a risky business, but I trust I will not hurt the feelings of any of my former students if I single out several who have been especially productive. The late Henry J. Browne (1919-1980) gave great promise with his notable volume, *The Catholic Church and the Knights of Labor* (1949), as he did in another area, archival administration, as the Catholic University of America's first archivist. Unfortunately, his biography of John Hughes (1797-1864), Archbishop of New York, was never finished, for the nine chapters that I read were far and away the best thing ever done on that important churchman. The work had been commissioned by Francis Cardinal Spellman (1889-1967), but the latter's practice of submitting the chapters to certain New York priests who had no real competence to judge their merit or demerits was a discouraging factor to the author. I do not mean to exonerate Harry of all blame in the matter, but had he received a really intelligent reaction to what he had written, I think he may well have completed the work. It was only one more instance of benighted interference by clerics in matters in which they had no real competence. In fine, what they wanted was what I have often called history as "moonlight and roses," with nary a mention of anything even remotely critical. The unfinished Hughes biography was but another in a series, for example, the life of John McCloskey (1810-1885), Hughes' successor in New York, allegedly written by John Cardinal Farley (1842-1918), but actually by Peter Guilday who told me that his manuscript was 'castrated'—Peter's own word—by Patrick J. Hayes (1867-1938), at the time Auxiliary Bishop of New York. It was decidedly not the way to promote history religious or secular.

A contemporary of Harry Browne's in my seminar, and his good friend and mine, was Annabelle M. Melville, a convert to Catholicism whose advent to the university in the late 1940's proved to be a real boon for American Catholic history. As a laywoman Annabelle won an almost unique status in the field with her splendid biographies of Elizabeth Seton, Archbishop John Carroll, and Boston's first bishop, Jean Cheverus. She continued her research and writing while teaching at Bridgewater State College, capping off this productive career after her retirement with the two-volume work, *Louis William Du Bourg, Bishop of Louisiana and the Floridas, Bishop of Montauban, and Archbishop of Besançon, 1766-1833,* (1986) which won the General L. Kemper Williams Prize of the Louisiana Historical Association. It is not an exaggeration to say that Annabelle Melville has been the most distinguished laywoman in the field of American Catholic history, a true adornment to the discipline in every sense of the word. It was, then, an altogether merited honor when in December, 1987, she was elected first vice president of the American Catholic Historical Association, the first woman chosen since the Association's founding in 1919. Thus she will automatically succeed to the presidency in 1989, the bicentennial year of the organized Catholic Church in this country.

About the time that Annabelle Melville was concluding her doctoral studies, there arrived Father Colman J. Barry, O.S.B., with his master's degree from Fordham University. Colman was one of the most imaginative students I ever had, creative, energetic, and resourceful. From the outset he was interested in the German Catholic immigrants, coming as he did from Saint John's Abbey in Stearns County, Minnesota, a solidly German settlement. After completing his course work he was off to Germany to do research and the final product, *The Catholic Church and German Americans* (1953) has continued to the present day as a seminal study in Catholic immigration history. Colman later published a first class institutional history to commemorate the centennial of Saint John's, edited a highly useful collection of documents,

Readings in Church History, not to mention a history of the Benedictine missions in the Bahamas, and an absorbing biography of one of the American Church's leading papal diplomats, *American Nuncio, Cardinal Aloisius Muench* (1969).

Another student who has more than made his mark is James Hennesey, S.J., for many years at Boston College and at present located at Canisius College in Buffalo. This gifted young priest was interested in the interchange between theology and history, a recurring theme in his writings and one that was featured in his impressive volume, *The First Council of the Vatican: The American Experience* (1963). Not only has Jim continued to do research and publish numerous articles in the quarter century since he took his doctorate, but he has proved a very popular lecturer who has drawn on his historical knowledge to enlighten the numerous audiences he has been invited to address. The distillation of that knowledge was produced in attractive dress when there appeared late in 1981 his latest book, *American Catholics. A History of the Roman Catholic Community in the United States,* by which I was honored for it had been dedicated to me. The choice in 1986 of James Hennesey as President of the American Catholic Historical Association was a tribute altogether fitting and richly deserved.

To be sure, there were others besides those mentioned above, others who gave genuine promise as future historians of the American Church, but who for one reason or another were prevented from fulfilling the role. I think of Patrick Ahern who died suddenly some weeks before his forty-ninth birthday after having produced two solid volumes as well as having brought the archives of the Archdiocese of Saint Paul-Minneapolis into working order for research purposes. There was also Oscar H. Lipscomb whose fine study of Catholicism in Alabama never saw the light due to his having been plunged into administrative tasks immediately after taking his doctorate in 1963, with the final eclipse for historical undertakings coming in November, 1980, when he was consecrated as first Archbishop of Mobile, his native city. He has, nonetheless, continued to lend strong support to Clio's cause in his capacity as a trustee of the Catholic University of America and of the North American College, Rome, while finding time to review an occasional book in American Catholic history and to maintain active membership in the A.C.H.A. and the historical society of Alabama. It has often seemed to me that an uncommon number of trained historians have been swallowed up by administration of one type or another, and thus deprived church history of their talents. A more recent example than that of Archbishop Lipscomb is Joseph P. Chinnici, O.F.M., of the Franciscan School of Theology, Berkeley, whose productive pen has been slowed by being elected vicar provincial of the friars' California province. I was happy to have had a minor part in his early graduate training when he took my course and seminar at the Graduate Theological Union in Berkeley in 1970. Joe's scholarly books and articles in the history of American Catholic spirituality have gone a long ways toward creating a new and long neglected aspect of the Catholic tradition in this country.

As I remarked above, the students in American Catholic history were never numerous even in the years before history in general suffered a severe decline. Yet a quarter century ago an analysis of the state of the discipline found the number of Catholic graduate students remarkably high. This study stated that in a sample of 182 candidates for the doctorate in history twenty percent were Catholic. These authors thought in general history students seemed to retain a religious affiliation more than those in other disciplines, and they added, "Notably more Catholic graduate students are found in history than in other disciplines."[1] I have taken no poll but

---

[1]Dexter Perkins, John L. Snell *et al., The Education of Historians in the United States* (New York, 1962) 42, 44.

I would seriously doubt that these data from 1962 would be duplicated today, for unless I am greatly mistaken history in general, and church history in particular, has experienced as marked a decline in Catholic circles if, indeed, not a greater downgrading than in secular institutions. I have more than once deplored the frequent rhetorical emphasis on the Catholic Church's historical character with so little done in certain Catholic universities, colleges, and seminaries to promote that history in a real or practical way. Church history remains for the most part a step-child even in some seminaries whose business is the instruction of the future clergy.

In the training of any scholar—be he or she an historian, a mathematician, or economist—the environmental factor is of importance. In all my teaching posts up to 1935 the responsible people were invariably kind and thoughtful, but they could do nothing to relieve the limited library resources of Atchison, Bourbonnais, Winona, San Rafael, and San Antonio. Even if the heavy teaching loads in those institutions had not prevented me from doing research and writing, I would have been handicapped by the lack of source material both manuscript and printed. In that regard Washington offered a very happy contrast and, in fact, the only thing about Washington that deterred me was the capital's summer heat and humidity, this in the years before air-conditioning had become common.

Apart from the availability of sources, the historian is improved or impeded by those with whom one works. In this respect I was very fortunate in my close association with historians of the caliber of Peter Guilday, Al Ziegler, Martin McGuire, and Leo F. Stock (1878-1954), all of whom were learned in their specialty and were generous and congenial in lending me help whenever I turned to them. To be sure, there was the occasional sharp difference of opinion both in the Department of History and the editorial board of the *Review,* but these tense moments were smoothed over and left no permanent scar.

On a higher plane of the chief executive officers of the university, my experience was more mixed. Of the nine bishops who served as rector—the term used until the late 1960's—I knew six, several only very slightly and several others fairly well. Between 1927 and 1943 my dealings with Thomas Shahan, James H. Ryan, and Joseph Corrigan were quite infrequent and of no really significant character. With the advent of Patrick J. McCormick (1880-1953) as rector in 1943, I came a bit closer to the administration. I say 'closer' in the sense that my personal research, and that of several of my graduate students, fixed upon the history of the Catholic University of America and thus inevitably brought involvement with the administration. I had started out originally to write a biography of John Lancaster Spalding, first Bishop of Peoria, the diocese in which I was born. A visit to Peoria, however, then revealed little if any manuscript sources, and I ended with scarcely more than a rather revealing visit with the late bishop's niece, Mrs. Mary Robb, a charming woman, indeed, but one who could not envision her uncle in any but the most flattering terms.

In this preliminary inquiry I found that in what sources there were, published or unpublished, Spalding's role as the principal *gratia agitans* of a Catholic university for the United States turned up repeatedly. I decided, therefore, to focus on Spalding and the university question which ultimately resulted in a detailed study of the university's early history which was published in 1946. Had I pursued the idea of a biography I might well have succeeded, but that need was later admirably filled by my student, David F. Sweeney, O.F.M., in his doctoral dissertation, *The Life of John Lancaster Spalding, First Bishop of Peoria, 1840-1916* (1965). Meanwhile I suggested to several of my students the successive university administrations as subjects for their master's theses, with the result that between 1948 and 1950 Patrick Ahern, Peter E. Hogan, S.S.J., and Colman Barry produced volume-length accounts that covered the regimes of John J. Keane, Thomas Conaty, and Denis O'Connell and were larger than many a doctoral dissertation, all being published by the university press.

In the course of my own research on the university's formative years I encountered sharp disputes and differences of opinion among the bishops and I told the story with candor in the thought that the unvarnished truth would best serve the cause, an attitude I passed on to my students in their histories of the university between 1889 and 1909. That brings me back to Patrick McCormick, rector at the time. He was a singularly placid person, tall, handsome, dignified, and enjoying the gift of serenity to such a degree that some wag said his motto might well be, *Semper paratus et numquam turbatus!* As might have been expected, the candid accounts of the books on the university aroused criticism in conservative quarters, for at that time we were still held firmly in the grip of the so-called ghetto mentality that, as I have previously remarked, considered this kind of history an altogether unnecessary and dangerous washing of the family linen in the public view.

Meanwhile what did Bishop McCormick think and do about it? The closest I ever came to finding out was when I visited his office and asked to examine some correspondence of Thomas Bouquillon (1842-1902), the university's first professor of moral theology, which for some unaccountable reason had been stored in the rector's desk. The permission was readily granted. I went through the documents, and as I was preparing to leave McCormick quietly remarked, "You know there has been some criticism of those books on the University." I replied, "Yes, I know," and thereupon took my departure never to hear another word about the matter from that quarter. Whatever deficiency McCormick may have revealed as a 'do-nothing' rector, and there was serious criticism of him on that score, the church historians had no reason for faulting him in their regard. My personal relations with Patrick McCormick remained cordial to the day he died of cancer in May, 1953.

My relationship with McCormick's successor, Bishop Bryan J. McEntegart (1883-1968), was of quite a different character. Following a decade as Bishop of Ogdensburg, he came to the university in June, 1953, where he served until April, 1957, when he was named Bishop of Brooklyn. Our initial relations were friendly although never close. When I was invited to give the Walgreen Lectures at the University of Chicago in 1954 I sought his permission, something I would probably not do today when that sort of thing has become far less common. He seemed happy at the news and with a quiet chuckle said, "I am glad you are not a Jesuit." Precisely what he meant, I did not know and did not ask.

About the same time there came an invitation from the American chairman of the International Congress of Historical Sciences, Myron P. Gilmore of Harvard, to read a paper on the Catholic Church and Church-State relations in the United States at the meeting scheduled for Rome in 1955. At the moment there was a sharp controversy in Catholic circles over this very question with John Courtney Murray, S.J. (1904-1967) on one side being vigorously opposed by two conservative theologians at the Catholic University of America, Joseph C. Fenton (1906-1969) and Francis J. Connell, C.SS.R. (1888-1967). My sympathies were entirely with Murray and I was eager to accept, while at the same time recognizing the delicate nature of the assignment by reason of the current controversy. Bishop McEntegart was in Europe when the invitation arrived, so I consulted the university chancellor who was also my own ordinary, Archbishop Patrick A. O'Boyle (1896-1987). The latter was quoted to me by his chancellor of the time, Philip M. Hannan, later Archbishop of New Orleans, to the effect, "He can be talked into this." Meanwhile the rector returned and shortly thereafter I was invited to lunch by O'Boyle when he asked that I forego the Roman lectures because of "Fenton and all that sort of thing," if I recall his words correctly.

While I was not specifically told by Archbishop O'Boyle that the rector had opposed my acceptance, I felt reasonably certain of this. In any case, there the matter rested until the spring of 1963 when McEntegart's successor, Bishop William J. McDonald, vetoed the students' invitation to four prominent theologians to lecture at the university, all of whom ultimately served as *periti* at Vatican Council II. It immediately became a *cause célébre,* and when I was asked by the editor of the weekly newspaper of the Diocese of Oklahoma City what I thought of the matter I answered that that sort of thing had been going on "at this university for a decade or more." The 'decade or more,' of course, went back to McEntegart's administration; he was furious and wrote me a scolding letter to which I replied only to be charged with being 'evasive.' I later learned that at the meeting of the Board of Trustees on April 24, 1963, McEntegart, "asked for a vote of reprimand for Monsignor Ellis,"[2] an action which was not, however, taken. One of my former students told me that a priest of the Diocese of Brooklyn had told him that the bishop did not wish the name of Ellis mentioned in his house.

The former rector's chagrin was understandable, and I was not free of blame for deliberately telling the Oklahoma editor that the *suppressio veri* by the university administration had gone back to McEntegart's time. Today the invitation to speak at the Roman congress would in all likelihood be accepted or declined without reference to either ecclesiastical or academic authority. But the 1960's were a different time in that regard, a time when ecclesiastical authority was much more heeded than it is in the 1980's. While on that subject,

---

[2]Minutes of the Board of Trustees, Book No. 5, Meeting of April 24, 1963, p. 389, Office of the President, The Catholic University of America.

this may be a good place to clear up a widespread rumor concerning my leaving the university in May, 1963, for San Francisco. My differences with the administration of that time were no secret, and that not only in regard to my open opposition to the banning of the four theologians but also to the editorial policies of the editor-in-chief of the *New Catholic Encyclopedia,* the offices of which were located on the campus with the editorial board drawn largely from the university faculty and alumni. In fact, I became so thoroughly disillusioned over the benighted policies of the editor-in-chief that I resigned as editor for the articles pertaining to American Catholicism. Meanwhile I had applied and received approval for a year's leave of absence—without salary—with the intention of taking up residence in San Francisco to write a book. Given the publicity that attended the fuss over the banned theologians, it was understandable that the rumor got out that I had been dismissed from the faculty. Nothing of the kind had occurred, although I was aware that the rector was glad to see me depart, and perhaps a few more than the rector! In any case, as I shall explain in due course I left the university for what was originally intended to be a single year but which turned out—like 'the man who came to dinner'—to be a stay of thirteen years.

Before describing my time on the Pacific Coast, I shall recount the intervening period which was one of the most rewarding of my life from several points of view. Having completed the book on the university, I was casting about for a suitable topic for future research and writing. I had meantime become a close friend of John K. Cartwright, first pastor of Immaculate Conception Church and then Rector of Saint Matthew's Cathedral. I did weekend work in both parishes after my ordination in 1938, hearing confessions, offering Mass, and preaching. Cartwright was a Baltimore-born man with an abiding esteem and love for James Cardinal Gibbons (1834-1921) in whose regime he had grown up, was ordained, and served. John was one of the best self-educated persons I have ever known, self-educated in the sense that he employed his superior mind by wide reading quite beyond the formal theological training he had received at Saint Charles College, Catonsville, and the North American College, Rome, where he was ordained in 1916 in the same class as the future Cardinal Spellman. On Saturday nights after confessions we would have prolonged conservations about all kinds of subjects, and when I told him of my desire to find a significant research project he had no hesitation in suggesting what that subject should be, namely, a biography of Gibbons. By this time (1945) I had become aware of Gibbons' importance and was a trifle awed at the thought of writing his biography. Cartwright, however, brushed this aside and said if I wished he would broach the subject with Monsignor Joseph M. Nelligan (1899-1978), chancellor of the Archdiocese of Baltimore who was in practical terms in charge of affairs during the repeated bouts of illness of the ordinary, Michael J. Curley (1879-1947).

In the sequel Joe spoke to the archbishop who gave his permission for access to the archives, and thus without further ado I embarked on what turned out to be my *magnum opus* on July 5, 1945, when I entrained for Baltimore. At first I was slightly intimidated by the gruff archbishop who came along shortly after I had begun, said he heard I wanted to write Gibbons' life, and then exclaimed, "I did not approve of Cardinal Gibbons. When I came here, I found the atmosphere saturated with liberalism!" But he quickly added that I had full permission to proceed, nonetheless. 'Fair enough,' I thought to myself, and it is pleasant to record that he was as good as his word and never intervened in the slightest way during the next two years before his death on May 16, 1947. When I went to Richmond in the summer of 1946 to work in the archives I told the Baltimore-born Peter L. Ireton (1882-1958), Bishop of Richmond, Curley's remark about Gibbons, whereupon

Ireton exclaimed, "It's a damn lie!" The loyalty of the Baltimoreans to Gibbons' memory was deep and enduring.

If the research for the book on the university's formative years had introduced me to some of the best archival depositories, the Gibbons biography drove home the indispensable character of archival research. Baltimore's manuscript collections were by far the richest I was to employ over the next three years, but I tried to cover every important depository I could find throughout the United States, for Gibbons' contacts were literally nationwide and, indeed, in relation to the Catholic Church, worldwide. In most cases I met with kind and co-operative treatment, although the actual condition of many of these archives was far from what is today demanded by the archival profession. Fortunately, the Baltimore collections which included 106 boxes of papers on Gibbons alone, had been reasonably well ordered and cared for over the years, as were those at the University of Notre Dame under the careful management of Father Thomas T. McAvoy, C.S.C. (1903-1969).

In fact, in only two dioceses was I turned away entirely, namely, Tucson where Bishop Daniel J. Gercke (1874-1964) was personally friendly but insisted they had nothing that would interest me—I would have been better satisfied in being allowed to determine that for myself! The second diocese was that of Savannah where in the absence of the bishop, Gerald P. O'Hara (1895-1963), a vicar general presided who was in anything but a good mood the morning I approached him. I tried to break the ice by saying it was a bad day in Savannah, to which he replied, "Every day in Savannah is a bad day for me." All entreaties ended in failure, and even the intervention of the charming Bishop of Charleston, Emmet M. Walsh (1892-1968), there that morning for a wedding in the cathedral, was unavailing. I have been informed by the present Bishop of Savannah, Raymond W. Lessard, that should I come that way again I would be warmly welcomed in the archives. As I write this, that fine archivist and good friend, Sister M. Felicitas Powers, R.S.M., is preparing to return to her native Savannah after a tenure at the Baltimore archdiocesan archives that has earned her the admiration and gratitude of any number of church historians. With Bishop Lessard and Sister Felicitas at the helm in Savannah, students will find a quite different reception than I encountered on that grim January morning of 1948.

The present knowledge and use of archives by church historians is today so universal that the topic needs no emphasis. In fact, the archival profession in both dioceses and in religious communities of men and women has made notable progress throughout the American Church, a development highlighted by the official statement on ecclesiastical archives issued by the National Conference of Catholic Bishops in November, 1974, in anticipation of the nation's bicentennial celebration. In that connection I recall the richest single find of manuscript sources which the late Harry Browne and I came upon in the summer of 1946 in Richmond, Virginia, when he was working on the Knights of Labor and I on the Gibbons biography. We were made very welcome by Bishop Ireton and by his chancellor, Justin D. McClunn. The latter casually remarked to us upon our arrival that he had been having a lot of amusement recently reading the O'Connell correspondence. Hearing this reference to the papers of Denis J. O'Connell (1849-1927), a pivotal figure in the history of the American Church from c. 1880 to 1920, we were immediately alerted. Justin told us he had come upon the collection in two old trunks in the attic of the chancery, whereupon the following morning Harry and I donned working clothes and proceeded to the attic! Here we found hundreds of letters to O'Connell during his tenure of the rectorship of the North American College, Rome, his rectorship of the Catholic University of America, and his episcopacy in San Francisco and Richmond. Dozens of letters in the last years of his life were unopened, Denis having apparently lost interest in it all. We reported our find to our professional colleagues, and in no time at all Tom McAvoy was in Richmond and got permission from Ireton to take the O'Connell Papers to Notre Dame, put them in order, make a copy, and return the originals to Richmond. They have since proven a rich quarry for many students of the period, and may well continue to do so for the indefinite future. When I say that O'Connell was one of the closest friends of Gibbons, it will be understood what this find meant to me.

When I recall how I traveled up and down the land from north to south and from east to west in search of every type of evidence about James Gibbons, there comes to mind Paul Horgan's absorbingly interesting presidential address before the American Catholic Historical Association in December, 1960, which he entitled "In Search of the Archbishop." Few people possess the talent of that gifted literary craftsman whose volume, *Lamy of Santa Fe* (1975) won him his second Pulitzer Prize, a biography of John B. Lamy (1814-1888), first Archbishop of Santa Fe. My prime concern in the time after July, 1945, might well have been termed 'in search of the cardinal,' which gradually became a labor of love as I assembled the data on the long and varied career of Baltimore's first cardinal. In that process oral history played its part in the sense of my conducting as many interviews with Gibbons' relatives and contemporaries as I possibly could, including two nieces and a nephew in New Orleans to say nothing of Baltimore clergy and several members of the Shriver family to whom the cardinal was closest of all his lay friends. During this period I had no leave of absence from my teaching and editing of the *Review,* but I used each weekend and summer first in the Baltimore archives and then in those of other centers like New York, Boston, New Orleans etc. Thus by late 1948 most of the evidence had been gathered and I was ready to begin the writing. In all, the work took seven years—three years of research, three years of writing, and a year to pass through the press.

At length the work was finished and appeared in November, 1952, in two large volumes totaling over 1,400 pages attractively boxed. The Bruce Publishing Company spared no effort by way of numerous illustrations, fine paper, good print, and widespread advertising. In general the work was well received, although it did not escape a harsh review in *The Commonweal* from an ardent admirer of John Ireland (1838-1918), Archbishop of Saint Paul, who thought the latter had quite outshone Gibbons in leadership of the American Catholic community. All things considered, this review by a Sister of Saint Joseph was more understandable than the course taken by Sir Shane Leslie (1885-1971) who first wrote a quite negative review in *The Tablet* of London, and then after receiving a remonstrance from Harry Browne, if I recall rightly, turned around and followed it with a highly complimentary assessment! I mention this to indicate the utterly arbitrary character of book reviews; they can make or break a book at times for the oddest of reasons, and the hapless author can do little or nothing about it. For that reason, save for a review the writer of which I know to be a thoroughly competent authority and a person of genuine integrity, I have long since come to take book reviews *cum granu salis,* whether the book in question be my own or one by someone else.

My research for the life of Cardinal Gibbons was extended to Europe by the happy circumstances of having been invited by Archbishop O'Boyle to accompany the Archdiocese of Washington pilgrimage to the Holy Year celebrations in April, 1950. The opportunity to visit Paris, Rome, London, and Dublin enabled me to investigate the archives of the Society of Saint Sulpice in Paris, those of the Congregation de Propaganda Fide in Rome, and the papers of Henry Edward Cardinal Manning, (1810-1892), Archbishop of Westminster, then housed at Saint Mary of the Angels, Bayswater, London. In all these depositories I found pertinent documents that shed further light on Gibbons' career. In Ireland I was warmly received by James Fergus, Bishop of Achonry, the diocese in which the Gibbons family lived. He had, in fact, kindly gathered data from the village of Ballinrobe and other local sources. James Gibbons had been born in Baltimore, but was taken to Ireland as a child when the family made a visit which lasted for some years, the father and one sister dying there of famine fever before Mrs. Gibbons and the remaining children came again to the United States and settled in New Orleans. I was deeply grateful to Bishop Fergus who as I write this is still living in retirement at the advanced age of ninety-one.

While the documents found in these European depositories were not great in number, they added significant details to Gibbons' activities, especially those in the Manning Papers. In a word, the biography would have been the poorer without them. Moreover, this trip enabled me to visit the Oratory in Birmingham for the first time where I was thrilled to be shown about by Father Henry Tristram, an authority on the life of John Henry Newman (1801-1890) who had become one of my heroes. When I told him that Gibbons had called on Newman in 1880 and taken breakfast with him, he led me to the table in the community refectory at which Newman always sat and said it was at this spot that they had had their visit. Gibbons later remarked, "I need not say with what keen pleasure I listened to the wealth of anecdote and narrative that flowed so abundantly from his well-stored mind."[3] It was a small matter, to be sure, but one of enduring memory for me, for of all the churchmen I have read about and studied I think I would say that Newman and Gibbons have been the two who have left the deepest impression on my mind and my heart.

If I were asked how it came about that I cultivated a love of Newman, the answer would touch on a variety of reasons.

---

[3]John Tracy Ellis, *The Life of James Cardinal Gibbons, Archbishop of Baltimore, 1834-1921* (Milwaukee, 1952) I, 198.

Early on, as the current expression has it, I was attracted by the man's sense of the real and the genuine in contrast to their opposites. The idea was expressed as well as I could phrase it by Tristram when he wrote of Newman:

> He was at once repelled by the slightest pretence or insincerity or humbug, and it was a strong condemnation from him, if he said, so and so is so unreal.[4]

Then there was for me the fascination of his English prose, for example, the famous sermon of "The Second Spring" preached at the English hierarchy's first plenary council in 1852. I have read it again and again, and every time I can scarcely hold back the tears so deeply am I moved by the lofty ideas so incomparably expressed. Repeatedly in reading Newman I have found him stating truths in language that I would have wished to employ but did not, which accounts for my frequent quotation of him in my own writings or in sermons and lectures.

Still another aspect of his writings that drew me was the man's profound sense of history. Newman had no professional training as an historian, but few historians have so caught the spirit of an age or a person, and conveyed it so vividly, as he did, for example, in *The Arians of the Fourth Century* (1833) and in pen pictures of people like Saint Athanasius *et al.* This was brought out by Thomas S. Bokenkotter in his Louvain doctorate in 1959, *Cardinal Newman as an Historian,* and has been featured by many who have written about Newman. In addition, I was attracted to him by the amount of suffering he had to endure at the hands of Catholic churchmen. True, he felt it keenly and revealed a highly sensitive nature, but Newman mustered more patience than most men would have been able to show

---

[4]Henry Tristram (Ed.), *Meditations and Devotions by John Henry Newman* (New York, 1953) xiv.

in the circumstances, and there came through to me a person of uncommon spiritual quality whose perception at times amounted to prophecy that was vindicated long after he had left this world, for example, the teaching of his essay on the development of doctrine (1845), on the position of the laity in the Church, and other matters that Vatican Council II strongly promoted to the point of some characterizing it as 'Newman's council.'

Finally, I confess Newman's most enduring attraction for me has relatively little to do with history. It has been rather the support and consolation I have derived from him in the things of the spirit, such as the unfailing inspiration for my life as a priest that has come from his spiritual writings, an inspiration that has proved greater for me than any other source save the New Testament itself. For example, I recently purchased the one-volume edition of the *Parochial and Plain Sermons* that first began to appear in 1834 and have gone through numerous editions. Here the eight volumes in one with their more than 1,700 pages are affording me daily reading that may well continue until I die, and for that handy single volume I am grateful to the Ignatius Press that brought it out.

I returned from Europe in June, 1950, the richer and the wiser for having gone in the sense that I now had a more enlightened approach to the Church's past, especially in those countries such as France, Italy, Switzerland, Germany, England, Scotland, and Ireland from which were sprung, so to speak, our American Catholic immigrant roots. I had seen portions of all those lands and felt something of their national ethos and mood, and that proved helpful when I later added a course in the history of European Catholicism since 1789 to my offerings in American Catholic history. For that enrichment I have always been mindful of the debt I owed to my ordinary, Cardinal O'Boyle, for having invited me to be his guest on that Holy Year pilgrimage, and this in spite of the fact that on occasion I spoke and wrote in a vein that put a certain distance between us.

Mutatis mutandis, the same could be said of my extended visit two years later to South America. In the spring of 1952 I received a call from Edward Miller, Assistant Secretary of State for Latin American affairs, who asked if he could come to see me. I had met him briefly at Saint Patrick's Church the previous autumn when I had preached, if I remember correctly, at the annual Pan American Mass. The purpose of his visit was to ask if I would make a tour of South America since, he said, most Latin Americans thought us Americans, 'Protestants and materialists.' He thought that if a Catholic priest who was also a university professor were to go there it might help to disabuse the South Americans of some of their mistaken impressions of us. I stated that I did not speak Spanish or Portuguese which I thought would be a major handicap, but Mr. Miller believed the prospective audiences understood enough English to render intelligible what I would say. As it turned out, I soon became aware that many in the audiences I addressed had come out to test their English, not to hear what Ellis might have to say about the Catholic Church in the United States, and everywhere I was met by people who pleaded with me to get them to this country.

In mid-June I flew out of Washington via Miami with the first major stop in Bogotá, the capital of Colombia. I want to guard against this account becoming a travelogue describing the next six weeks; yet it is not irrelevant to the theme of this memoir, for my knowledge of the Church's history was broadened by this direct contact with a region of which I had heretofore only the most superficial acquaintance. No historian of the Church could very well be indifferent to such memorable buildings as the venerable cathedral of Lima, capital of Peru, and in the same city the tombs of Saints Rose of Lima and Martin de Porres. And so it continued through

Santiago, Chile, Buenos Aires, Argentina, Rio de Janeiro and São Paulo, Brazil, and Montevideo, Uruguay. Having come under the auspices of the Department of State, I was in the capable hands of the various cultural attachés of the respective American embassies. All went as scheduled save in Buenos Aires where I was informed by the attaché who met my plane that I should enjoy myself in the Argentinian capital since the current anti-American spirit would not permit of any lectures. At the time Evita Peron, the president's wife, was dying and feeling ran high with the American cultural center having been bombed the previous week. Buenos Aires was my first and only experience of living in a police state where several Americans would ask if I had my police pass, and then warn me, "For God's sake do not lose it." An American Redemptorist priest called at my hotel to see me and as we chatted in the lobby he quietly said, "May we go to your room?" When we reached the room and the door was closed he said, "I am sorry, but it was unsafe for us to be talking as we were in the lobby." Even in Rome in the days of the Fascists I had experienced nothing quite like the atmosphere in Buenos Aires. The trip on the whole, however, was an eye-opener for me in many ways that brought me for the first time into direct contact with the appalling poverty of the masses of the people, for example, in the *favelas* on the mountain side of that dazzlingly beautiful city of Rio de Janeiro or in the slums of Santiago to which the Holy Cross Fathers took me during my days in Chile. In a sense this was history in the raw, and the impression left in my mind is still vivid after the passage of over thirty-five years.

As I glance back over the years it becomes evident that the 1950's and the early 1960's were the period of my most productive writing and publication. Shortly after the appearance of the Gibbons biography I received an invitation from my friend, Jerome G. Kerwin (1896-1977), professor of political science in the University of Chicago, to deliver the annual Walgreen Lectures there. I decided on a general approach to the history of American Catholicism in the thought that that might be the most suitable for that audience. Preparation of these lectures during the closing months of 1954 was interrupted from time to time by the fact that my mother was then dying of leukemia which called for my presence at home and, in fact, she was buried only forty-eight hours before the first lecture was scheduled for January 24, 1955. If they were generally well received, they did not fail to draw criticism in certain quarters as being 'defensive' in tone. In any case, they were thought acceptable for publication as a volume in the series called the Chicago History of American Civilization edited by Daniel J. Boorstin, then a professor at the University of Chicago and later Librarian of Congress, who told me at one point that *American Catholicism* (University of Chicago Press) was the best seller in the series. When Jim Hennesey's general history of Catholicism in this country came out in 1981, the sale of my own book took a downward course as was to be expected. Yet to my surprise it had a comeback during 1985 when the press reported on August 15, 1986, that 748 copies had been sold during the previous year, roughly three times the number for 1984. I have remained at a loss to account for this increase, gratifying as it was. In all the work has sold to date (July, 1987) 34,181 copies, far and away the highest sales of any of my books. I would like to think that the higher sales represent an increase in courses being given in the subject in seminaries and colleges, but I have no real evidence to support that supposition.

About the time that the Walgreen Lectures were delivered, I received another invitation that ultimately led to the most widely publicized—and perhaps criticized—of all my written works. Father William J. Rooney, then Director of the Catholic Commission on Cultural and Intellectual Affairs, asked me to give a paper at their annual meeting scheduled for Maryville College, Saint Louis, in May. I told him I had some very strong views regarding Catholics' failure to do justice to the intellectual apostolate in this country, but he encouraged me to speak out with complete freedom. I entitled the essay, "American Catholics and the Intellectual Life," which appeared first in *Thought,* the Fordham University quarterly, that autumn, and then in book form in the next year with a foreword by John Wright (1909-1979), then Bishop of Worcester. I can honestly say that I had no idea that I had stirred such a widespread and animated reaction. I received several hundred letters from all over the nation, the majority in agreement, even if they were not all as strong as the former Jesuit provincial who wrote from New England, "For God's sake, keep on shouting. . . ." But all were by no means in agreement—far from it—and I was roundly scolded by a few for exposing our weakness to the public eye. My own ordinary, the Archbishop of Washington, was uneasy about the fuss that had been raised, and meeting me one day by accident on the campus said, "You had better let it rest for a while." I am in no position to judge the ultimate influence of this controversial item, but it was certain that the sixty some pages of the book edition caused more of a hubbub than the nearly 1,400 pages of the life of Cardinal Gibbons ever did—or ever will in the reprint of that lengthy work that appeared in the fall of 1987 from Christian Classics, Inc., of Westminster, Maryland.

In the excitement over *American Catholics and the Intellectual Life* my other publication of 1956 got lost to view except for the professionals in the field. That was the first edition of *Documents of American Catholic History,* a work which has just come out in its fourth edition in three handsome volumes from Michael Glazier, Inc. The idea for the *Documents* was owed to Colman Barry, my imaginative graduate student, who urged me on and said the seminar students would help in the gathering of the documents which in due course they faithfully carried out. All in all, I think the *Documents* was one of the most useful things I ever did, that is, useful for teachers and students of the American Catholic past.

The unconscious 'provoker' of my next book was that charming fellow, Father John J. Sweeney (1923-1965), Superintendent of Schools of the Diocese of Peoria, whose life was cut short by a tragic automobile accident. John induced the diocesan superintendents of schools to assemble in Peoria for the first of their annual meetings outside the city of Washington, and then, in turn, he induced me to preach the sermon at the opening Mass in Saint Mary's Cathedral and suggested Peoria's first bishop, John Lancaster Spalding, as a possible subject. It was an altogether appropriate suggestion given Spalding's leading role in the history of Catholic education in the United States. The sequel was its publication in book form as *John Lancaster Spalding, First Bishop of Peoria, American Educator* (1961), the National Catholic Educational Association's Gabriel Richard Lecture for that year. Almost from the time that I knew what a bishop was, I had been intrigued by Spalding who confirmed my mother and whose name was heard frequently at Saint Viator College and was not unknown in my native town of Seneca.

During these same years I published a considerable number of articles both scholarly and popular, but I will make no further mention of them here, since an admirably complete bibliography of all my writings from my first feeble efforts as a high school senior and college freshman writing in the school's journal, *The Viatorian* (1923-1924) down to the year 1985 was compiled by Mark A. Miller of the Diocese of Rochester and published in the *Festschrift* for my eightieth birthday.[5]

[5]Nelson H. Minnich, Robert B. Eno, S.S., and Robert Trisco (Eds) *Studies in Catholic History in Honor of John Tracy Ellis* (Wilmington, Delaware, 1985) 674-738.

As I come to the close of this chapter that has included accounts of my travels abroad I think of Hilaire Belloc's association of the two, travel and history, in an essay called "The Old Things." I am perfectly aware of Belloc's deficiencies as an historian, but it does not follow that because he was heedless of original sources and careless about accuracy of detail that he wrote nothing of value for historians. For that reason I find in his words the expression of what I felt in a vague way from my time in Europe and Latin America. He put it this way:

> Those who travel about England for their pleasure, or, for that matter, about any part of Western Europe, rightly associate with much travel the pleasure of history; for history adds to a man, giving him, as it were, a great memory of things—like a human memory, but stretched over a longer space than one human life. It makes him, I do not say wise and great, but certainly in communion with wisdom and greatness.[6]

---

[6]A.N. Wilson, *Hilaire Belloc* (London, 1984) 151.

CHAPTER IV

San Francisco and Rome

Like many another visitor to the city by the Golden Gate, long before Tony Bennett's famous song had been heard, I had lost a part of my heart to San Francisco. I am far from having seen all the great cities of the world, but of those I have seen only one, in my judgment, outshines San Francisco, namely, Rio de Janeiro. There is more to it than its beautiful bay and beyond the Golden Gate Bridge the brown hills of Marin County. San Francisco's charm embraces as well its colorful history, the spirit of its friendly inhabitants, and the cultural riches such as its splendid opera and the intellectual stimulation of its distinguished institutions of higher learning in the neighboring cities of Berkeley and Stanford, to name only two. I first came in contact with much of this in the summers of 1933 and 1934 when, as I have said, I taught at Dominican College in San Rafael.

What, the reader may ask, has all this to do with the career of a church historian? Nothing directly, I must confess; yet my California years played a role in my life as an historian as I shall try to explain. When, therefore, I decided to take a year's leave of absence with the idea of writing a general history of American Catholicism, there was little doubt about where I would spend that year. A further factor in choosing San Francisco was the large number of its Catholic priests

71

whom I had come to know, for the Archdiocese of San Francisco in those years sent more graduate students to the Catholic University of America than any other diocese in the country. Through one of these students, Mark J. Hurley, later Bishop of Santa Rosa, I had come to know Monsignor Thomas F. Millett (1893-1964), pastor of Saint Agnes Church. Mark's prediction, "You two will hit it off very well," proved to be altogether accurate. Tom Millett was an avid reader of church history and ecclesiastical biography which established an immediate and lasting link between us. Thus when he offered me hospitality in his rectory I readily accepted his invitation. It was a wonderfully genial household where, I was told, the influence of Millett with two successive archbishops, whom he had served as secretary, Edward J. Hanna (1860-1944) and John J. Mitty (1884-1961), assured him that he would have the best of clerical assistants, and they were, indeed, a superior group of priests, including my dear friend, Raymond G. Decker.

When I left Washington in May, 1963, I had no idea that it would be thirteen years before I would again reside in the national capital. As it turned out the multi-volume history of the Catholic Church in this country that I had envisioned never got written, in part, as I said, because the San Franciscans were too sociable and I was too weak. But all that first year was not spent with evenings at the War Memorial Opera House, although it was there I acquired my taste for Verdi and Mozart operas, and with trips to Lake Tahoe or Carmel and Monterey. My host had a room fitted up for me just off the church and there I managed to get written the first volume of what I intended would be a series covering the entire history of Catholicism in this country. *Catholics in Colonial America* (1965) was the only one in the projected series due to the fact that the more I thought of it the less was I attracted to the idea of a multi-volume work of this kind. That was the first product of my time in San Francisco, but another book, *Perspectives in American*

Catholicism, was published shortly after I had made my move to the Pacific Coast, a fact that I noted by the following inscription in my copy, "San Francisco, August 19, 1963." It was a collection of essays, sermons, radio talks, etc., I had been urged to bring together by Colman Barry for a series called Benedictine Studies. In that book I cherish especially the foreword written by my lamented friend, Paul J. Hallinan (1911-1968), first Archbishop of Atlanta.

Among San Franciscans whom I had known quite well before I lived there was John B. McGloin, S.J., of the University of San Francisco, who was an active member of the American Catholic Historical Association and a frequent reviewer of books on California history for the *Catholic Historical Review.* Unknown to me, John had suggested to the USF administration that I be invited to join their faculty. I received a call from Charles W. Dullea, S.J., the president, and during my visit he made me an attractive financial offer, stated that the teaching load would be relatively light, and added, "We would like you to continue your research and writing," or words to that effect. Given my love for San Francisco, the presence there of a good number of friends, and my discontent with the administration of the Catholic University of America of that time, it did not take me very long to decide to accept. As it turned out, in September, 1964, I entered upon a period of twelve years on the USF faculty during which I was treated with the utmost generosity and kindness by the Jesuit administrators and their lay associates. For example, the university rented an apartment for me in the immediate neighborhood, paid the first year's rent, and invited me to take my meals with the Jesuit community in Xavier Hall for which I was not charged a penny. On the personal level, therefore, my affiliation with the University of San Francisco left nothing to be desired.

Academically speaking, I felt the lack of graduate students to direct, although my classes in the history of the Church were well patronized up to near the end of my time in San

Francisco. In fact, I had some excellent undergraduate students such as Harry B. Morrison and Michael Galligan as well as Suzanne Lee and her brother David, once again to risk the naming of names, for there were other good students as well who later went on to become priests, teachers, lawyers, etc. Meanwhile I quietly applauded the decision to have the Department of History retain its basically undergraduate program with a modest effort to grant a limited number of master's degrees with no doctoral program in history. In this regard USF was realistic and free from the pretense of offering academic programs for which it was not equipped. I was an occasional reader on a master's thesis, but during my twelve years there no candidate for church history appeared on that level.

Residence on the Pacific Coast enabled me to widen my acquaintance with historians of that region, among whom none proved more profitable than the friendship I developed with Raymond J. Sontag (1897-1972) who after a distinguished career at Princeton was in 1941 named Ehrman professor of modern European history in the University of California, Berkeley. As Secretary of the American Catholic Historical Association I was ever on the alert to increase the membership, and when I learned Sontag was a Catholic I wrote to congratulate him on his conversion and to invite him to become a member. In his characteristically forthright way Ray answered that he could not accept my congratulations, he was not a convert to the faith, he had been born and raised a Catholic, had lapsed but had then returned to the fold. In due time he was elected President of the Association for 1952 and remained a member until his death.

I came to know this outstanding historian really well through the family of Michael and Mary Cummins whose two priest sons, Bernard and John, had grown close to the Sontags after John enrolled in one of Ray's courses with a view to earning a master's degree in history at Berkeley. Many an evening we would assemble around the Cummins table in their modest home on Woolsey Street in Berkeley where Ray would enlighten the company by his incisive comments and critical views on the passing scene with apposite references to historical events and persons. He was a general favorite with both colleagues and students, and I recall seeing in *Time* in an article on the university at Berkeley his picture with the caption beneath "SRO," 'standing room only' in his classes. It was an impressive fact borne out when one night while dining in San Francisco a former student asked him how many students he had, to which he replied, "About 750." When asked if there was a classroom large enough to accommodate such numbers Ray said there was not such, they were sitting on the window sills, on the floor, and on the stairways! It was all described in the modest tone and spirit that characterized this man of genuine integrity, a true professional who had gained a national, if not international, reputation as a specialist in the history of modern Germany, a Catholic layman who was at the same time a daily communicant and a model man of the Church. Add to this a steady stream of books and scholarly articles and one could appreciate Ray Sontag's influence both within and without the professional circles in which he moved with such ease. His final book, *A Broken World, 1919-1939* appeared as Volume XIX of the Rise of Modern Europe series in 1971, the finale to a truly distinguished career that came to a sudden end in October, 1972, leaving all of us in his debt both for his professional competence and the example of his manly piety.

I considered myself fortunate to have known Ray Sontag very well in the last decade of his life. His friendship lent support to my own undertakings in Clio's cause as it had done from our earliest acquaintance, and that in the same manner in which my first years as secretary of the A.C.H.A. and editor of the *Review* found reassurance in the strong backing of Carlton J.H. Hayes (1882-1964), the famous Columbia University historian and authority on the history of nationalism, a convert to Catholicism who remained a stalwart man of the faith from the day, as I once heard him say, when he read Cardinal Gibbons' *Faith of Our Fathers,* and as he expressed it, "heard the call." It is not easy to convey to others how much the support of mature historians like Sontag and Hayes meant to me—and there were others—in the years when I was trying to find my way in professional circles a half century or more ago.

When an historian writes a memoir dealing with his or her professional life it may well be expected that it will include a treatment of the historian's philosophy of history. In that regard I find myself somewhat at a loss, for I must confess that aside from acceptance of the basic rules governing sources such as preference for original rather than secondary evidence, an attempt to tell the story as honestly and objectively as possible, I had no real philosophy concerning the discipline. I must, then, for the most part fall back on the old axiom, *Nemo dat quod non habet.* That is doubtless the reason why J. Douglas Thomas in his article on historians of American Catholicism entitled the section on me, "Eclectic Church History: John Tracy Ellis,"[1] I found the analysis of my work by this Texas Protestant balanced and fair. He could hardly have been expected to find a distinct philosophy in the writings of one who has never been conscious of possessing such. That does not mean that I have been aware of deliberately evading the issue; it is just that I have written with a view to setting forth the facts in the matter, whether that be a movement, an institutional development, or the life of a person. That being true, I am fully conscious of having researched and written with the purpose of throwing light on the past of the Catholic Church, both here and abroad, and that with no apologetic aim but rather, as I have said previously, with as much candor and objectivity as I could

---

[1] J. Douglas Thomas, "A Century of American Catholic History," *U.S. Catholic Historian* 6 (Winter, 1987) 41-48.

bring to the subject. That I have failed in some respects to achieve that goal has been evident from the charge made by several critics that I have been 'defensive' in my attitude toward the Church. I know of no historian who has entirely escaped criticism on one score or another, and I have not been an exception to that general rule.

I have more than once entertained a scruple that I was quoting too much in my writings, for I have myself been critical of others on that score, especially certain bishops who have made their pastoral letters and addresses a tissue of quotations from the reigning pope. Yet all of us come across in our reading expression of ideas that so aptly state what has been in our mind that we yield to the temptation to quote at some length. At a time when I was a child of eight an English historian of high promise, George Peabody Gooch (1873-1968), published a volume called *History and Historians in the Nineteenth Century*. Forty-five years later (1958) Gooch brought out a revised edition of that work in which he noted the great advance that the discipline had made in the intervening period. I felt so much kinship with what he wrote there that I want to quote Gooch as having said what I should like to have said. Contrasting the standard of scholarship in 1913 with that of 1958, he found the latter definitely higher. ''We are less cocksure, less dominated by prejudices, less prone to plausible generalisations,'' he remarked, and then continued:

Our inspiring ideal and our paramount obligation is to deserve the unstinted confidence of our readers. As Ranke declared in a memorable phrase: 'the writing of history is a matter of conscience.' No strident advocate of his race, his country, his party or his church, has a claim to enter the temple of Clio. If I were asked to draw up Ten Commandments for historians I should put at the top: 'Remember your moral responsibility to your readers.' Historians, like other people, are creatures of flesh and blood, and the author's personality will always peep through the printed page: but we must do our utmost to play fair, to understand the life of distant times and ideas which we do not share. No student should base his conception of such controversial themes as the Reformation and the French Revolution on a single writer or a single book, for in some spheres where our deepest feelings are involved full agreement is too much to demand. All I ask is that scholars should regard themselves, not as gladiators struggling in the arena amid the plaudits of their respective supporters, but as a band of brothers dedicated to the single-minded pursuit of truth.[2]

Those words written five years before I moved to San Francisco embody much of my quite inchoate philosophy of history. I do not pretend that I have achieved their ideal; I can only say that I have tried.

Upon moving to San Francisco I joined the Pacific Coast Branch of the American Historical Association and attended its meetings with some regularity. My friend, Ray Sontag, had been elected its president in 1959 and remained active up to his retirement from his professorship in Berkeley. It was in that group, if I recall rightly, that I came to know Moses Rischin, a Jewish scholar who taught American social history at San Francisco State University, and a number of other historians of the Pacific Coast. I cannot now remember who it was that invited me to give a paper at their annual meeting at the University of Santa Clara in late August, 1968. In any case, I entitled the paper, "The Ecclesiastical Historian in the Service of Clio," which treated my concept of the church historian's role in general social history, the needed relation of ecclesiastical to secular history, and certain experiences I

---

[2]G.P. Gooch, *History and Historians in the Nineteenth Century* rev. ed. (Boston, 1958) iii.

had encountered as an historian of American Catholicism, etc. This paper came about as close as I have ever come to outlining my philosophy of history, or more particularly, the philosophy that should guide an historian of the Church. I quoted from Lord Acton, Philip Hughes *et al.* to illustrate various points, and in order to enter a light touch now and then I cited the lifelong pursuit of George Gordon Coulton (1858-1947) of Cambridge who spent a fair portion of his career tracking down dishonest statements of medieval historians of the Church. Coulton had found an especially egregious offender in Andreas Agnellus, Bishop of Ravenna, who about 850 embarked on a series of biographies of the occupants of his episcopal see. The Cambridge historian quoted the following from Agnellus with understandable relish:

Where I have not found any history of any of these bishops, and have not been able by conversation with aged men, or inspection of the monuments, or from any other source, to obtain information concerning them, in such a case, in order that there might not be a break in the series, I have composed the life myself, with the help of God and the prayers of the brethren.[3]

Historians of a far less biased mind than that of Coulton would be sorely tempted not to pass up this extraordinary description of one's historical method!

The paper read at Santa Clara in August, 1968, was a product of what one might call the after-glow of Vatican Council II. Before that secular and interdenominational audience I tried to illustrate the better climate of opinion for religious history with examples drawn from the aloof attitude

---

[3]John Tracy Ellis, "The Ecclesiastical Historian in the Service of Clio," *Church History* 38 (March, 1969) 113, citing G.G. Coulton, *Medieval Panorama* (New York, 1938) 439.

of the past in contrast to the more open approach of the late 1960's. We are even today—two decades later—far from having achieved the ideal in that regard, but the ecumenical movement has improved the writing of religious history in many ways, most of all, I think, by opening the windows of the minds of historians to the positive features of other religious traditions than their own, and that has been a notable gain for Clio and her disciples whose main preoccupation is the history of the things of the spirit.

Upon the approach of Vatican Council II I received an invitation from Robert E. Tracy (1909-1980), Bishop of Baton Rouge, to accompany him to the council as his *peritus.* He stated that he believed an historian of the American Church should be there to view the historic gathering at first hand. To be sure, it was an attractive prospect and I agreed, made a down payment on my plane ticket, and then changed my mind. Why? It was a mixture of motives that combined obligation to my classes, my inability to speak Italian or Latin, and a puzzlement concerning how I would spend my time at Rome. Bob Tracy was generous in his understanding of my change of mind, and that was the end of the matter for the time being.

Meanwhile I followed the council closely from its opening in October, 1962, principally through *The Tablet* of London, for the San Francisco *Chronicle* and *Examiner* were less than satisfying in their coverage of the council, and *The Monitor,* the weekly of the Archdiocese of San Francisco, was not much better. My historical sense was roused by the sharp encounters between critics of the Roman Curia, such as the cardinals of Cologne and Lille, and Cardinal Alfredo Ottaviani, the stern watchdog of the Holy Office who more than lived up to his motto, *Semper idem.* All the while I continued to give lectures and sermons here and there as well as to assemble a series of papers I had written on the education of priests which were published by Fides Publishers, Inc. of Notre Dame in 1967 under the title,

Essays in Seminary Education, a topic that has been of major interest to me through most of my mature life.

As the fourth and final session of Vatican Council II neared I received an invitation from Bishop Francis F. Reh, Rector of the North American College, Rome, to deliver a series of lectures to the students on the history of the Catholic Church in this country. This time I accepted without any hesitation, feeling that I could spend my time profitably in an assignment of this kind and simultaneously see something of the council in action. Those weeks of September, 1965, were among the most memorable and pleasant of my life. The students were receptive and curious enough to ask some challenging questions, and the social life of the college was of more than ordinary interest with the Cardinal Archbishops of Saint Louis and Boston and their attendants at table. It was there that I came to know quite well Joseph Ritter (1892-1967) and Richard Cushing (1895-1970) with whom I felt quite at home from the outset, for neither cardinal took himself too seriously, a prime quality in my reckoning. Both men were admirably open-minded after the pattern of Pope John XXIII who had set the tone, so to speak, for the council, even if his basically conservative nature would have drawn back from some of the interpretations placed on the council's documents in the aftermath of the gathering.

Since my lectures were in the evenings it left me free to attend the council in the mornings when Bishop Reh and I would go together in his car to Saint Peter's Basilica. The most memorable day for me was September 21, 1965, when the Declaration on Religious Freedom received its over-whelming vote of 1,997 to 224. The conservatives had fought it bitterly to the very end, but Paul VI remained loyal to his promise at the end of the third session that this issue would be the first order of business in the final session. I recall taking my place in the tribune for Mass and seeing Amleto Cardinal Cicognani, Secretary of State, hobbling across the floor to his place. I thought nothing of it, merely concluding that the old churchman was late for the session. I did not learn until later that the pope had sent for him and several other die-hards to inform them that there would, in spite of their opposition, be a vote on the declaration that day. It was in every sense a dramatic event with stirring interventions from both sides, the most notable being, I think, that of Josef Cardinal Beran (1888-1969), exiled Archbishop of Prague, whose eloquent plea for religious freedom came with singular grace from one who had spent years in prison in defense of that principle at the hands of both the Nazi invaders of his country and then after 1948 at the hands of the Communist usurpers.

The more than 2,000 bishops in the aula that day sensed the significance of this man's witness as they broke into applause as he mounted the podium. Beran spoke with great feeling about the unhappy effects that followed a denial of religious freedom, and calling history in defense of his position he declared:

> Everywhere, and always, the violation of liberty of conscience gives birth to hypocrisy in many people. And, perhaps, one can say that hypocrisy in the profession of the faith is more harmful to the Church than the hypocrisy of hiding the faith, which anyway is more common in our times.
>
> So, in my country, the Catholic Church at this time seems to be suffering expiation for defects and sins committed in times gone by in her name against religious liberty, such as in the fifteenth century the burning of the priest John Huss and during the seventeenth century the forced re-conversion of a great part of the Czech people to the Catholic faith, under the rule 'whoever's territory it is, that also is his religion.'[4]

---

[4]Josef Cardinal Beran, "On Religious Liberty," English translation quoted by John Tracy Ellis, *A Commitment To Truth* (Latrobe, 1966) 61-62.

Neither before nor since have I ever been present at an event where history was made before my eyes as that September day of 1965. It was an hour of special meaning for me as an historian of the American Church, recalling as I did the long years of suspicion with which non-Catholic Americans had quite understandably viewed the Church's teaching on union of Church and State *vis-à-vis* the American principle of separation of the two. My entire time in Rome that year was memorable in every respect, but no day measured up, historically speaking, to the council's action on September 21. Here, indeed, was history in the making, and I have always been grateful that I had the privilege of being there to witness it in person.

To state that Rome is perennially interesting is to belabor the obvious, and that is especially true for the historian of the Church. I had learned much on my two previous visits to the Eternal City, but nothing to equal my stay in 1965 when the council had brought virtually the entire American hierarchy to the city, to say nothing of the hundreds of bishops from almost every country in the world. Here for the first time in nearly 2,000 years the Catholic Church's alleged universality became real, and that in itself was an awesome sight for the historian.

While all of this was true, other obligations beckoned back in San Francisco. I remember how shocked Archbishop John J. Maguire of New York seemed when meeting me on the plane he learned that I was not stopping in New York for Pope Paul VI's visit there on October 4 to address the United Nations. Nor did he appear satisfied when I said I had my classes to teach at USF; even my gesture in buying him a cocktail during our stopover in Gander was not enough to overcome his puzzlement at a professor of church history failing to avail himself of an opportunity to be present for so historic a happening.

Apart from the duty to resume my teaching, I had incurred other obligations that were then coming due. Among these was the Wimmer Lecture at Saint Vincent College, Latrobe, which I had decided to devote to the subject of honesty and truthfulness with a survey of notable violations of the same in the Church's history and the harmful results that followed. The lecture was later published in book form with the title, *A Commitment To Truth* (1966), and when Ray Sontag read it he wrote to say he thought it was the most important thing I had done since the life of Cardinal Gibbons. I felt no lack of solid evidence for my central theme, but I was at pains to show the happy consequences of honesty and truthfulness in the lives of certain churchmen in order to balance the negative exhibits. In that regard I was able at the outset to profit from the widespread admiration for Pope John XXIII whose death only a year and a half before had produced worldwide grief the essence of which, I thought, had been caught by a simple poem of Edith Lovejoy Pierce in the leading Protestant weekly, *The Christian Century*. It read as follows:

> HISTORY, with its reversals,
> Cannot wreck this tomb.
> Here is no image to be disenthroned.
> Here is no myth to be destroyed.
> This life was too plain, too clear;
> Too many people saw the smiling truth
> For any future raid to steal such honor.
> No sentry need be posted,
> No watchman set to guard
> The tomb that is a hundred million hearts.[5]

More than twenty years later I still find that poem a striking tribute to a life of personal integrity, embodying in poetic verse a lesson that is timeless in the affairs of humankind.

---

[5]Edith Lovejoy Pierce, "Pope John XXIII. In Memoriam," *The Christian Century* LXXX (June 26, 1963) 823.

From the beginning of his pontificate in 1958 I shared the love of 'a hundred million hearts' for Pope John, an affection that was deepened by my knowledge that he was once a professor of church history in his diocesan seminary in Bergamo. For that reason and others I shall always be grateful to Peter Hebblethwaite for his splendid biography, *John XXIII, Pope of the Council* (1984).

While still in Washington I gave a course in modern English and Irish Catholicism beginning with the age of the Tudors and coming down to the twentieth century. In San Francisco I decided to broaden the offering to European Catholicism since 1789, an addition to my regular courses in American Catholicism. This variety served me well when I was invited to be a visiting professor at Brown University (1967), at the University of Notre Dame (1970), and at the Gregorian University, Rome (1974). I found that the necessary reading in European religious history gave depth and greater meaning to the American Catholic story, and I have continued to the present day to offer these courses in alternate semesters with the American version always drawing roughly double the number of students as the European which, I suppose, is to be expected in that most of us are more interested in our own past than we are in the past of other peoples.

Fortunately, a lifelong love of reading served me well in this endeavor. I have tried to keep reasonably abreast of recent scholarship by reading such works as *The Church in a Secularised Society* (1978) by Roger Aubert *et al.,* Owen Chadwick's *The Popes and European Revolution* (1981), the pertinent volumes of Hubert Jedin and John Dolan (Eds.), *History of the Church,* to mention only an item or two. At the same time I have demanded roughly 200 pages of collateral reading per week from my students until in recent years when I found they were predominantly seminarians with very heavy course loads that seemed to call for cutting the assigned readings in about half. At the beginning of each semester I acquaint students with the demands for collateral reading and make clear that there will be a monthly written test since, as I tell them, we are all at heart Scarlet O'Haras, who when confronted with an unpleasant prospect would say in Margaret Mitchell's *Gone With the Wind,* "I will think of it tomorrow." At times students have grumbled at the reading assignments, but normally they have accepted them with resignation, and now and then one has in after years thanked me for having demanded this reading. Meanwhile I have tried to let no significant book in church history go by without at least a scanning acquaintance, and in some instances a careful and close reading by reason of its high merits, for example, two current works, Eric O. Hanson's *The Catholic Church in World Politics* (1987) and Owen Chadwick's *Britain and the Vatican during the Second World War* (1986), a fascinating account in every respect. I must desist, however, lest this become a tiresome listing of titles that will serve no purpose.

The visiting professorships in which I served since 1967 have widened my acquaintance with fellow historians, even if they may not have added anything very specific to my historical knowledge. In all these assignments the invitation came quite 'out of the blue,' as it were with one exception. That was my appointment as scholar-in-residence at the North American College, Rome, during which I taught at the Gregorian University (1974) and later at the Angelicum (1976). In this instance I solicited the appointment by asking my good friend, Monsignor George G. Higgins then residing in Rome for the three-month institute for continuing education of American priests, if he would inquire about the possibility of an opening there. Shortly thereafter I received a letter from Bishop James A. Hickey, then Rector of the North American College, saying 'a little bird' had whispered in his ear, and he gladly accepted its suggestion that I should be appointed scholar-in-residence beginning in September, 1974. In taking this initiative I was motivated by my desire to live at Rome for more than a few weeks in order to profit from its incomparable cultural and religious resources and to savor its rich historical heritage. By the time I reached Rome in September James Hickey had been named Bishop of Cleveland, but his successor, Monsignor Harold P. Darcy—and his staff—made me very welcome.

For the first semester I lived at the Casa Santa Maria, the original site of the College in downtown Rome, where there resided around seventy priest graduate students from the United States along with thirty some American priests enrolled in the institute for continuing education. It was a highly congenial company for whom I gave that winter a series of lectures on the history of American Catholicism at the invitation of the chairman of the house committee, Thomas J. Barry of the Archdiocese of Hartford, with whom I became good friends. And Tom was only one whose friendship I then made and have retained to the present; in that regard I think of Martin Connor of Boston, David Givey of Philadelphia, Edwin O'Brien of New York, and Brother Randal Riede, C.F.X., who for over a decade and a half has exercised an extraordinary influence on the seminarians and priests of that community.

At the outset I had about thirty students in the course at the Gregorian University where, as I recall it now, all but a priest from Yugoslavia who lasted only a few days, were Americans seeking to know more about their own history. While I lived at the Casa it was very easy since it was practically next door to the Gregorian, but when I moved to the College on the Janiculum in February, 1975, it was something else, and the effort to have the course taught at the latter raised problems for the Gregorian administration that were only reluctantly solved by them allowing me to continue to teach off the premises and the students still get credit for their work at the Gregorian. If the site caused difficulty, the antiquated administration of the library at the Gregorian gave more serious trouble, for it seemed that they almost defied one to check out a book, even to have stack privileges. In the end I had to depend more and more on the limited resources of the library at the Janiculum where Brother Randal's unfailing co-operation was always a source of consolation and joy for this 'foreigner' in their midst.

During that academic year the late Monsignor Luigi Ligutti (1885-1983) once the ranking person in the Catholic Rural Life Conference of the United States and later long resident in Rome, arranged a detailed tour of the Vatican Archives where Monsignor Charles Burns, a native of Scotland, was generous with his knowledge and time in showing me through the vast collections. My memory may be playing tricks on me here, but I seem to remember that he said there were thirty-five miles of shelving in this world famous depository. I had, of course, known of the prime importance of the Vatican Archives for historians of the Church, but this tour brought out in a vivid way the immensity and variety of the documentary collections. I remember being told that the removal of the archives of the Apostolic Delegation (since 1984 the Apostolic Nunciature) in Washington from its founding in 1893 to 1939 were so numerous that they created a real problem of space, to say nothing of processing the documents for practical use.

When one realizes that the Holy See maintains representatives in approximately 130 countries with each accumulating documents almost daily one can envision the problem it creates for the limited staff of the Vatican Archives as this voluminous flow moves into that depository. It is small wonder, then, that although Pope John Paul II has opened the archives down to the death of Pope Benedict XV in 1922, it does not follow that they are immediately ready for scholars' use. And across town are housed the archives of the Congregation de Propaganda Fide (known since 1967 as the Congregation for the Evangelization of Peoples) which governed the Church in the United States down to 1908 and there are thousands of documents relating to American

Catholic history. When I visited the Propaganda archives, the splendid work of the Academy of American Franciscan History in compiling the multi-volume series entitled *United States Documents in the Propaganda Archives. A Calendar* was of great assistance. The value of a closer acquaintance with these rich depositories for the historian would not need to be emphasized, a value that only Rome could provide.

My year and a half in Rome—I returned in late January of 1976 for the second semester of the academic year, 1975-1976—was a time of personal enrichment in more ways than visits to ecclesiastical archives. It afforded me the opportunity to attend notable liturgical events such as the midnight Mass of Pope Paul VI in 1974 when he opened the Holy Year of 1975. Likewise I was happy to accept the invitation to preach in the Church of Santa Maria in Trastevere, the titular church of Cardinal Gibbons, and there to note his famous sermon on taking possession of that basilica on March 25, 1887. To stand in the same pulpit from which he had delivered his memorable address on the relations of Church and State in the United States meant much to me, as it did to be invited to be the principal celebrant and homilist when the North American College community assembled in Saint Peter's for a Mass at the chair.

True, these events added nothing very special to the training of the church historian as such, but the memory of the historic happenings in these venerable churches was not lost on me and helped to render more real and lively my instruction to students at a later date. Then there were the convivial gatherings that often accompanied these liturgical functions, such as the cocktail hour and dinner at the Casa on Thanksgiving Day when Rome's American colony kept high festival, along with a few non-American guests. On one occasion there was present Paolo Cardinal Marella (1895-1984), Archpriest of Saint Peter's Basilica. Someone said to me that he wished to speak to me, so I went over, paid my respects, and for want of anything better to say remarked, "You served in the Orient at one time, did you not?" He answered that he had, indeed, served in Korea and Japan, and then added the extraordinary intelligence, "Korea is a peninsula and Japan is a chain of islands." I confess that this reply left me with nothing further to say as I bowed and moved off wondering if that sort of thing was typical of his kind, or was it merely the cardinal's notion of the discretion one should employ in conversing with visiting Americans.

There is an obvious difference between a memoir and a travelogue and I do not want to blur that difference here. Yet I should like to mention several other trips taken during my time in Rome, travels that helped to fill in my historical knowledge about places of major significance in the history of the Church. Practically all of these sojourns were organized at the Casa Santa Maria with the company consisting of from thirty to twenty or less priests who availed themselves of the opportunity to see something of Poland and Soviet Russia on one trip and of the Holy Land on another. It was my first venture into eastern Europe, and in all likelihood it will have been my last. The weather in March, 1975, was cold and forbidding in both Poland and Russia, but that did not prevent us from seeing a good deal of Warsaw, Czestochowa, and Kraków with stops coming and going at historic spots such as the home of Frédéric Chopin and the Franciscan monastery of Saint Maximilian Kolbe (1894-1941), the friar who had given his life as Auschwitz to save the life of the father of a family. To have stood at the monastic cell of Father Kolbe at Niepokalanow and to have done the same before his tiny cell in the concentration camp of Auschwitz, was a moving experience I shall always remember.

A good deal of Warsaw, of course, had been destroyed during World War II, but much had been rebuilt, for example, Saint John's Cathedral. As I gazed up at the pulpit I thought of the many times the voice of Stefan Cardinal

Wyszyński (1901-1981) had resounded there in defense of the
Church's rights against the Communist government. And in
the cathedral of Kraków I caught my first glimpse of Karol
Wojtyla as the cardinal archbishop washed the feet of the
men during the Holy Thursday liturgy, little suspecting,
needless to say, that I was gazing at one who less than four
years later would be elected pope. Our visit to Auschwitz was
a sobering experience, the memory of which one will carry to
his grave.

In the Russian capital we visited the traditional places such
as the Kremlin, and on Easter Sunday I had the privilege of
being the principal celebrant and preacher at Mass in Saint
Louis Church, the only center of public worship for
Catholics in the city. A highlight of the trip was our visit to
Zagorsk where we were given lavish hospitality by the monks
of this headquarters of the Russian Orthodox Church. I
heard that a rumor got out that we were a delegation from the
Vatican which may have accounted for the warmth of our
reception, although the rumor was quite false. In any case,
our reception was exceptionally warm with the bountiful
luncheon and even the final toast offered by one of the
monks when he lifted his glass and said in Russian, "One for
the road!" We made a number of stops at Russian Orthodox
churches in which we found numerous worshippers,
predominantly women of middle age or older, although there
were also a sprinkling of younger people. In both Poland and
Russia the number of intoxicated people met in the streets
exceeded anything I had experienced elsewhere, although one
could walk those same streets in safety which was something
one could no longer do in most American cities. Leningrad
proved to be much more attractive than Moscow with its
palaces and government buildings from the imperial regime,
the most notable being the Hermitage with its superb
collection of paintings.

A trip to the Holy Land was no less rewarding the
following year, and a number of side trips out of Rome were
helpful to the historian, for example, to Ravenna for the

famous mosaics, to Florence for its art treasures and centuries-old buildings of both Church and State. In a word, my travels during the three semesters I taught in Rome were a real boon by way of the visual images created which enabled me to concretize in a more realistic fashion the lectures that I later gave in the course on European Catholicism since the French Revolution.

In this memoir I have tried to make clear what have been the most influential factors in shaping my life as an historian, in my case an ecclesiastical historian. Outstanding teachers who sparked the initial interest were there at the outset, study habits formed under their guidance played a major role, availability of resources, that is, archives containing manuscript materials and libraries with well stocked secondary works and scholarly periodicals, travels that shed light on historical persons and places, the inspiration supplied by superior students eager to learn content knowledge and the best methods to acquire a professional efficiency—all these, and others, entered into the process, as I am sure, every historian would attest. Beyond these tangible goals lay a more subtle factor, namely, love of the discipline. The idea is embodied in Pascal's famous axiom, "The heart has its reasons, which reason does not know. We feel it in a thousand things."[6] We do, indeed, and if that 'feeling' is lacking something very basic has gone out of the enterprise.

I can honestly say that my heart was in full accord with my head as I pursued my historical training; in other words, I never felt like Saint Paul who quoted the Master as telling him at that dramatic moment on the road to Damascus, "It is hard for you, kicking like this against the goad."[7] From the time that I understood the process, that is, the gathering of facts, the rules of interpretation of those facts, the necessity of prolonged labor in research, writing, and publication, and

---

[6]L. Brunschvieg *et al.* (Eds.), Pascal *Pensées*. (Paris, 1914) IV, 277.
[7]*Acts* 26: 15.

last but by no means least, the best pedagogical methods to impart this knowledge to others in the classroom, I have felt happy in what I was doing. I have had a good measure of success in teaching, a fact which, I hope, I can express with no overtones of pride or arrogance. When the temptation arises to think well of myself on that score, I ask myself: 'Where did your ability to teach come from?' And that question prompts the reminder of Jesus' words in the Sermon on the Mount, "Your light must shine in the sight of men, so that, seeing your good works, they may give the praise to your Father in heaven."[8] I see no virtue in denying one's talents since they have been God-given, and by the same token I see no reason for trying to hide our deficiencies, for example, my lifelong inability to make any progress in foreign languages.

While writing this chapter I have been reading the summer 1987 issue of *Notre Dame Magazine* where I found my good friend and fellow historian of the Notre Dame faculty, Philip Gleason, asking Father Edward A. Malloy, C.S.C., the new president:

Do you see any change, anything new or different, in the impact on teaching of the enhanced emphasis on research?

I found the president's reply to that question an admirable summing up of what I have tried through sixty years to practice in my life as an historian. The president answered:

If faculty members are not engaged in *both* teaching and research, if they are not continuing to learn themselves

---

[8]*Matthew* 5: 16.

and taking it into the classroom, then they are not doing their jobs.[9]

That is a high yet attainable goal for any teacher, a goal that the historian of the Church can keep before his or her eyes as they strive to advance Clio's cause.

[9]"A Presidential Conversation," *Notre Dame Magazine* 15 (Summer, 1987) 16. Pope John Paul II made the same point in addressig the theologians at the University of Salamanca on November 1, 1982, when he said: "It is silent, self-denying labor, requiring of you full dedication to research and teaching. For teaching without research runs the risk of falling into routine and repetition." See *Origins* 12 (November 18, 1982) 368.

CHAPTER V

". . .To Labor Until Evening Falls."

Old age has for me brought more meaning to the psalmist's words, "Man goes forth to his work to labor until evening falls." (*Psalm* 104). I have never been less happy than when there was seemingly nothing to do, a state of mind that may well have arisen from my failure in early life to develop hobbies, to participate or interest myself in sports, or to find any particular pleasure in leisure time. Whatever the cause, work has been a salutary factor in my life, and in that regard I am a firm believer in the old adage, 'An idle mind is the devil's workshop.' Especially has this been true since I entered upon my twilight years when the pressing duties of life have slackened and I have found myself with more time on my hands. Although I frequently quote the words of Henry Edward Manning, Cardinal Archbishop of Westminster, concerning his declining years, "I am slowing into the terminus," I have welcomed the 'slowing' as a gradual process, not one that would find me fully retired with little or no incentive left in life. It was reasons of this kind that prompted me to accept the request that I write this memoir.

To do anything useful for one's self or for others a prime necessity is good health, and in that regard I have been singularly blessed, with only a relatively mild case of diabetes to contend with these past twenty years. When, therefore, I received an invitation in the spring of 1976 to be the first occupant of the Catholic Daughters of the Americas Chair of American Catholic History at the Catholic University of America, I gladly accepted President Clarence Walton's offer. I was then in my twelfth year of teaching at the University of San Francisco where all had gone well for about a decade until the Department of History there, as in most institutions of higher learning, experienced a marked decline of patronage. During my first years as USF I had enrollments of from twenty to thirty students, but by 1976 they had fallen off to around five or six in each course. It was a signal that my best days there had passed and that it was time for me to move on, although the administration gave no indication of terminating my contract on that account.

The invitation to return to Washington was thus a welcome one, for at the age of seventy-one I had few options for further employment. But it was not merely a matter of expedience or convenience, for there was no institution that meant more to me than the one where I had received my graduate training, and no city where I preferred to dwell more than the national capital. My place of residence for the first semester was determined almost by accident. I was invited to participate in the consultation held in the spring of 1976 at Sacramento for Detroit's Call to Action Congress scheduled for the autumn of that year. There I met Bishop James S. Rausch (1928-1981), then General Secretary of the National Conference of Catholic Bishops, who invited me to live at the staff house on 14th Street, N.E., only a few blocks from the university campus. I accepted his invitation and spent a very pleasant four and a half months under that hospitable roof where I enjoyed the company of the twenty some priests employed by the United States Catholic Conference.

The obligations of the occupant of the Catholic Daughters' chair consisted of a lecture course, a seminar, and a single public lecture. For some reason that I cannot now recall the public lecture was delayed and was not delivered until March 25, 1979, on the subject of my experiences at the university from my advent there in 1927 to 1979. It was later published in the spring 1979 issue of *Social Thought.* During that semester I helped direct several candidates for the master's degree and served as a reader on dissertations, in this regard resuming academic tasks that had been part of my routine before my time in San Francisco, none of which, to be sure, added anything very distinctive to my role as a church historian, but it helped to put me in the swing of things, so to speak, while meanwhile I continued to serve as an advisory editor of the *Catholic Historical Review.*

As the semester came to a close I received a visit from the Rector of Mount Saint Mary's Seminary in Emmitsburg, Maryland, Father Harry J. Flynn, now Coadjutor Bishop of Lafayette, Louisiana, and our mutual friend, Father William J. Fay, professor of Scripture at Emmitsburg. They invited me to join the Mount Saint Mary's faculty, an offer which I accepted for a semester as a visiting professor. I had known a good deal about that historic institution founded in 1808, but realizing, as I later told them, that I was a 'hopeless urbanite,' I felt it would be unwise for me to commit myself to a permanent stay in that altogether beautiful but rather isolated rural setting. As it turned out I had a very enjoyable semester in Emmitsburg where the large class of more than fifty students kept me busy, and where the company of Harry Flynn, Bill Fay *et al.* was highly congenial.

Before leaving Washington for Emmitsburg I raised the question with the Department of Church History about my returning there and teaching a course for my board and room. I was not then, nor am I now rich, thank God, but I had sufficient income that I did not need a salary. Moreover, I noted that they lacked a course in the history of European Catholicism since the French Revolution. My suggestion was adopted and has proved a very agreeable arrangement during the last ten years. On August 13, 1977, I moved into 101 Curley Hall the day Colman Barry left it to return to

Collegeville after his deanship of the School of Religious Studies. I have never been happier and more pleasantly situated than during the last decade in this beautiful apartment with the chapel one floor down where the Blessed Sacrament is reserved, and excellent meals served in the Curley Hall dining room. It is no wonder that several have remarked on my situation, for it has, indeed, been literally ideal. With the agreement of my colleagues I have since 1977 offered a course of three hours a week, one semester in American Catholicism and the alternate semester in European Catholicism with the former usually drawing about twenty-five students and the latter ordinarily attracting half that number or less.

Such, then, in outline have been my academic commitments since leaving San Francisco. At the repeated request of John Cardinal O'Connor, Archbishop of New York, I served as a visiting professor at Saint Joseph's Seminary, Dunwoodie, from September to December, 1986. The cardinal's extraordinary kindness to me since we first met in July, 1984, has been such that I felt I owed him this service as a token of appreciation. In all likelihood the months in New York were my final visiting professorship as I feel more and more inclined to remain at home and forego change of residence and travel. It is all, I suppose, part of the 'slowing' process mentioned above.

It is now more than twenty years since I first published an autobiographical article to which I have already made reference. I have also previously touched on my philosophy of history or the lack thereof. I should like to quote here a few lines from that article of January, 1965, by way of a finale on my approach to the discipline of history in general and to church history in particular. These lines will, I hope, convey my concept of what history should always strive to be and to do. I then wrote:

I confess that I always shied away from too pronounced a 'Catholic' philosophy of history during my editorship of the *Catholic Historical Review,* and for that matter, in all that I have written as an historian, lest the apologetic approach should give it a coloration that would do a disservice to historical truth. . . .I need hardly say that I fully share the philosophy of all the *Review's* editors, past and present, in positing the existence of a divine providence in the affairs of men, and a special divine guidance over the Church which Christ founded to continue His mission in this world. But I do likewise believe that grave damage to Catholic scholarship has been done by some Catholics in the field of history who have viewed their task as a sort of battleground whereon they were called to fight the Church's foes and to defend her against their assaults.

I then cited a paper read in July, 1906, by a priest professor at a meeting of the Educational Conference of Seminary Faculties as a sample of the kind of thinking that I deeply deplored. This author declared that the fathers of Vatican Council I's constitution, *Dei Filius,* had clearly indicated "the apologetic value of history," and he then concluded:

History must be the weapon of defense, which, at all times, useful, is especially necessary in our times, when the enemies of the Church are arming themselves with all instruments of attack that can be found as fabricated by those who devote themselves to historical research.

To that quotation I added, "I have always been left unconvinced by this kind of approach, when I was not outright repelled."[1] I might remark here that the intervening

---

[1]John Tracy Ellis, "Reflections of an Ex-Editor," *The Catholic Historical Review* L (January, 1965) 471-473. The 1906 paper cited was by Daniel J. Kennedy, O.P., "The Importance of History in the Study of Dogma," *Catholic Educational Association. Report of the Proceedings and Addresses of the Third Annual Meeting, Cleveland, Ohio, July 9, 10, 11 and 12, 1906* (Columbus, 1906) 252.

years have deepened that conviction, and it is a pleasure to
record that my successors in the editing of the *Catholic
Historical Review* have shared that attitude and have
maintained a breath of view that has insured the journal
against a narrow ecclesiasticism, all of which, I trust, has a
relevance for the cast of mind with which I have tried to
pursue my work as an historian of the Church.

As I come to the close of this memoir I have asked myself
what I might add that would have some value for present and
future historians of the Church. Frankly, I can think of
nothing of a very original character, but perhaps I can speak
of a few matters that have been a serious concern to me in
relation to the discipline. Among these I would put near the
top the danger of attempting to say something new and
'exciting,' to employ that very tired word, at the expense of
sound judgment and common sense. In that regard I have
more than once quoted Paul Horgan's observation to the
effect that "Fashion in artistic and intellectual theory is
always fluid, new catchwords are born every year, and
nothing is more pathetic in its deseutude than the intellectual
or social chic of yesterday."[2] That says it is in a far more
elegant way than I could do, and expresses my mind
precisely. I do not intend to demean original thought or
expression, far from it; I mean only to deplore the strained
effort to say something new when there is no warrant for the
exercise, an effort that at times results in distorting history
instead of advancing the truth it is presumed to serve.

That history has genuine merit in helping one to weight
human endeavor, there is no doubt. David Knowles put it
well a generation ago when he declared:

It is, or should be, one of the great gifts of a study of
history that the superficial differences, the changing

---

[2]Paul Horgan, "The Abdication of the Artist," *Proceedings of the
American Philosophical Society* CIX (October, 1965) 270.

garments of the centuries, are not mistaken for changes of substance and essence.

In the same vein the learned authority in English monastic history went on to remark how the passage of years helps to bring to the person what he called, "the wisdom of experience and long observation; the expectations and despairs of earlier years are replaced by a saner estimate and a more sober hope."[3] It was this temper of mind that prompted Benjamin Franklin at the close of the Constitutional Convention to note that there were features of the document with which he then disagreed to which he added:

> But I am not sure I shall never approve them. . . . For having lived long, I have experienced many instances of being obliged by better information or fuller consideration, to change opinions even on important subjects, which I once thought right, but found to be otherwise. It is therefore that the older I grow, the more apt I am to doubt my own judgment, and to pay more respect to the judgment of others.[4]

Every historian could profit from that sage advice regardless of his or her age.

Old age has mellowed some historians after the pattern of Franklin, but it has found others soured and at times embittered toward those with whom they have differed. Michael Ramsay, former Archbishop of Canterbury, found this to be true in reading the lengthy memoirs of Hensley Henson wherein, he said, "friends who had known him best,

---

[3]David Knowles, "The Need for Catholic Historical Scholarship," *Dublin Review* CCXXXII (Summer, 1958) 123.

[4]Catherine Drinker Bowen, *Miracle At Philadelphia, The Story of the Constitutional Convention May to September 1787* (New York, 1986) 255.

felt that these volumes gave a distorted picture through passages of irritable self-justification and caustic criticism of contemporaries."[5] It is a threat to some that is not easy to overcome when they have found their works denigrated by fellow historians, for not all of us, alas, have the spiritual strength to rise above pettiness of this kind and to practice the principle enunciated by William Ewart Gladstone in his controversies with Henry Edward Manning when he told the latter:

> Our differences, my dear archbishop, are, indeed, profound. We refer them, I suppose, in humble silence to a Higher Power.[6]

One of the worst examples of this kind appeared in the autobiography of the distinguished English historian, A.J.P. Taylor. A reviewer of Taylor's *A Personal History* conceded that the latter had been treated shabbily at Oxford by not being offered the Regius professorship and by the history faculty terminating his lectureship in international history. "The trouble is," said the reviewer, "there is too much vanity in his ripostes." Taylor claimed he was by far the best of the eleven people who got firsts in history at Oxford in 1927, to which the reviewer commented, "It is perfectly true; it would still have been better left to others to say it."[7] I have known one or more church historians in my time who sailed perilously close to Taylor's frame of mind about themselves and their superiority to contemporaries, but let the axiom *'De mortuis nil nisi bonum'* obtain.

---

[5]Michael Ramsay's review of Owen Chadwick, *Hensley Henson* in the *Times Literary Supplement,* August 19, 1983, p. 878.

[6]Gladstone to Manning, February 25, 1875, in: Edmund Sheridan Purcell, *Life of Cardinal Manning, Archbishop of Westminster* (New York, 1896) II, 478.

[7]Robert Skidelsky's review of A.J.P. Taylor, *A Personal History* in the *Times Literary Supplement,* May 27, 1983, p. 540.

As I write these lines in late August, 1987, the media are busily preparing for the arrival of Pope John Paul II for his second visit to the United States. That event has set off a round of inquiries from reporters of all kinds with questions about the reason for his coming and about what he will say. I have tried to make it clear to these people that I am an historian, not a prophet. Once the historian begins to play the prophet he or she immediately jeopardizes their professional obligation, for it seems to me that truth has been stood on its head time and again by the so-called futurologists. And when it is attempted by historians they can look foolish, indeed, for example, when Will and Ariel Durant, authors of so much solid and sensible history, allowed themselves to venture the following:

> In the United States the lower birth rate of the Anglo-Saxons has lessened their economic and political power; and by the year 2000 the Roman Catholic Church will be the dominant force in national as well as in municipal or state governments. A similar process is helping to restore Catholicism in France, Switzerland, and Germany; the lands of Voltaire, Calvin, and Luther may soon return to the papal fold.[8]

It would be difficult to find a single valid point in those sentences written twenty years ago. The Catholics are today practicing birth control at almost the same rate as non-Catholics in this country, and far from showing a restored Catholicism in France the ancient faith there is

---

[8]Will and Ariel Durant, *The Lessons of History* (New York, 1968) 23. Thinking of the Durants' title, I am reminded of the words with which the leaders of Japan and the seven industrial powers opened their final communique at Bonn on May 3, 1985: "We have learned the lessons of history." Washington *Post,* May 4, 1985, p. A 12.

languishing at an alarming degree. So much for prophecy, a pasttime that the historian should be at pains to avoid.

It is easy for one in his eighties to take himself with unwarranted seriousness since too many of his contemporaries believe that age has endowed him with a wisdom denied to those younger than he. Here and there, now and then, one encounters an aged figure who answers to this concept, but in general those who have passed three score and ten are not much wiser than the rest of humankind. I have often thought that one helpful safeguard is to learn to laugh at oneself which, as I see it, is one of the most effective remedies for pomposity. A touch of lightheartedness is also salutary, for example, the kind of humor revealed by Belloc when he wrote:

> When I am dead
> I hope it may be said:
> 'His sins were scarlet,
> But his books were read.'

Some time ago a fellow historian and friend remarked that I had more than once said, 'Clio is a jealous mistress,' to which he added, "It might be good to indicate how jealous." It is not exactly easy to reply to that suggestion in a helpful way. What I have had in mind is the necessity of self-discipline if one espouses the life of a scholar, of reconciling oneself to the fact that a good many attractive features of every day living have to be passed up, for example, social gatherings, concerts, receptions to mention only three perfectly legitimate pasttimes. Why? For the very simple reason that there is not enough time in any one's life to indulge in productive research and publication and simultaneously take in the numerous diversions by which virtually every educated person is surrounded.

By no means am I suggesting that the man or woman who sets out to be a scholar must resign oneself to becoming a recluse or hermit. A certain amount of diversion is even necessary for a healthy existence, but it must be kept within limits and not allowed to rob one of precious hours for work. What I am saying here will not, I am sure, be thought odd to those whose lives are being lived in academia, for each has known and seen promising young persons start off with great expectations, and then witnessed a slow crumbling of the lofty ideal as the lives of these people become more and more distracted by activities in themselves good but leading up roads remote from the paths that lead to genuine achievement. Here, then, is my answer to my friend's suggestion of spelling out 'how jealous' Clio—or the muse of any discipline—may be if enduring results are to follow from one's efforts in any line of endeavor.

If the 'slowing into the terminus' in recent years has meant a slackening in publication of large and original books, the summer and autumn of 1987 have been occupied in part by the preparation of a fourth edition, revised and enlarged of one work, and the reprinting of a second. For the former I am beholden to Michael Glazier for having brought out the handsome three-volume edition of *Documents of American Catholic History* which, at the publisher's insistence, contained the two lengthy pastoral letters of the American bishops on nuclear warfare (May, 1983) and the American economy (November, 1986). I owe the reprinting of the life of Cardinal Gibbons, an expensive undertaking to be sure, to the initial suggestion of my friend, Monsignor George G. Higgins, who unknown to me approached John J. McHale of Christian Classics, Inc., who accepted the suggestion and spared no effort to have the biography of 1952 reproduced in an attractive dress. I can only hope that these publishers are more than repaid for their willingness to incur such an obligation at a time when the cost of publishing books of any kind is notoriously high. While I would not wish to preclude the possibility of any future writing in the history of American Catholicism, a sense of realism prompts me to think that the volume, *Catholic Bishops: A Memoir* (1983), and the two works mentioned above probably mark the end of my productive career. In this as in so many other circumstances of life I will simply say: *Videbimus.*

I am conscious of the fact that in the time ahead I may have reason to regret omissions of one kind or another in this memoir, as I have in other things I have written. I have tried to recall accurately those persons, places, and things that most influenced me in my life as an historian. Yet even now I think of certain people not previously mentioned, for example, Monsignor Philip Hughes (1895-1967) whose learned books in church history I had read long before we first met, and whose friendship I enjoyed and profited from during the last decade or so of his life. Philip was excellent company, a gifted story-teller, an ecclesiastical historian whose thorough research and balanced judgments won him widespread respect in the historical profession. He had been shamefully neglected by his own in his native England. I recall his telling me that when the American Catholic Historical Association bestowed on him the John Gilmary Shea Prize in 1954 for his multi-volume work, *The Reformation in England* (1950-1954), it was the first such honor he had received. I shall always be grateful to the University of Notre Dame for having added Philip to its faculty in 1955 and for having treated him with real generosity during his declining years. My final visit with him took place in June, 1967, when I was at Notre Dame for the commencement of my nephew, John. By that time he was bed-ridden and he died four months later. Friendships like that with Philip Hughes have been an immense boon in my life, and that both as an historian and as a person.

The late twentieth century is an age of profound revolution in virtually every aspect of life—political, social, and religious. It is a condition that reminds me of a description written a generation ago by Robert R. Palmer when he defined it in these terms:

By a revolutionary situation is here meant one in which confidence in the justice or reasonableness of existing authority is undermined; where old loyalties fade, obligations are felt as impositions, law seems arbitrary, and respect for superiors is felt as a form of humiliation; where existing sources of prestige seem undeserved, hitherto accepted forms of wealth and income seem ill-gained, and government is sensed as distant, apart from the governed and not really 'representing' them. . . .⁹

Needless to say, the late 1980's do not match this description in every particular; but there are sufficient similarities to make one pause. It is scarcely exaggerating to say that our current society has brought on widespread anxiety on the part of thoughtful people who sense that a remedy must be found somewhere if, as Palmer phrased it, "continuing deterioration is to be avoided. . . ."

I confess that at the moment I find it difficult to see a light on the horizon of national life, to discern a leader of the caliber and integrity of George Washington, Abraham Lincoln, or Robert E. Lee, for it seems to me it is that type of leadership that the United States desperately needs as the 1980's come to a close. Meanwhile, however, I refuse to succumb to a defeatist attitude, since I recognize and believe that hope is one of the theological virtues ranked with faith and charity. And when I experience momentary discouragement about the future of the United States and the world, I find reassurance in the history of the Church whose nearly twenty centuries in this world have borne striking witness through crises infinitely worse than the one through which we are at present passing to the words of the Master, "Know

---

⁹Robert R. Palmer, *The Age of the Democratic Revolution, A Political History of Europe and America, 1760-1800.* (Princeton, 1959) 21.

that I am with you always; yes, to the end of time.''[10] With his profound historical sense Newman read that message clearly in the Church's story. Let the cardinal, then, have the final word in expressing a belief and a hope in which I fully share and with which I take my leave:

> This is a world of conflict, and of vicissitude amid the conflict. The Church is ever militant; sometimes she gains, sometimes she loses; and more often she is at once gaining and losing in parts of her territory. What is ecclesiastical history but a record of the ever-doubtful fortune of the battle, though its issue is not doubtful? Scarcely are we singing *Te Deum,* when we have to turn to our *Misereres:* scarcely are we in peace, when we are in persecution: scarcely have we gained a triumph, when we are visited by a scandal. Nay, we make progress by means of reverses; our griefs are our consolations; we lose Stephen, to gain Paul, and Matthias replaces the traitor Judas.
>
> It is so in every age; it is so in the nineteenth century; it was so in the fourth. . . .''[11]

---

[10]*Matthew* 28: 20.

[11]John Henry Newman, *Historical Sketches* (London, 1906) II, 1.

INDEX